The
Neuropsychology
of Aggression

ADVANCES IN BEHAVIORAL BIOLOGY

Volume 1 • BRAIN CHEMISTRY AND MENTAL DISEASE
Edited by Beng T. Ho and William M. McIsaac • 1971

Volume 2 • NEUROBIOLOGY OF THE AMYGDALA
Edited by Basil E. Eleftheriou • 1972

Volume 3 • AGING AND THE BRAIN
Edited by Charles M. Gaitz • 1972

Volume 4 • THE CHEMISTRY OF MOOD, MOTIVATION, AND MEMORY
Edited by James L. McGaugh • 1972

Volume 5 • INTERDISCIPLINARY INVESTIGATION OF THE BRAIN
Edited by J. P. Nicholson • 1972

Volume 6 • PSYCHOPHARMACOLOGY AND AGING
Edited by Carl Eisdorfer and William E. Fann • 1973

Volume 7 • CONTROL OF POSTURE AND LOCOMOTION
Edited by R. B. Stein, K. G. Pearson, R. S. Smith,
and J. B. Redford • 1973

Volume 8 • DRUGS AND THE DEVELOPING BRAIN
Edited by Antonia Vernadakis and Norman Weiner • 1974

Volume 9 • PERSPECTIVES IN PRIMATE BIOLOGY
Edited by A. B. Chiarelli • 1974

Volume 10 • NEUROHUMORAL CODING OF BRAIN FUNCTION
Edited by R. D. Myers and René Raúl Drucker-Colín • 1974

Volume 11 • REPRODUCTIVE BEHAVIOR
Edited by William Montagna and William A. Sadler • 1974

Volume 12 • THE NEUROPSYCHOLOGY OF AGGRESSION
Edited by Richard E. Whalen • 1974

The Neuropsychology of Aggression

Edited by

Richard E. Whalen

Department of Psychobiology
University of California
Irvine, California

PLENUM PRESS • NEW YORK AND LONDON

Library of Congress Cataloging in Publication Data

Main entry under title:

The Neuropsychology of aggression.

(Advances in behavioral biology; v. 12)
Based on papers presented at a workshop sponsored by the Dept. of Psycho-
biology, University of California, Irvine, and held at Newport Beach, Calif., Mar.
1974.
Includes bibilographies and index.
1. Aggressiveness (Psychology)—Congresses. 2. Aggressive behavior in ani-
mals—Congresses. 3. Neuropsychology—Congresses. I. Whalen, Richard E., ed.
II. California, University, Irvine. Dept. of Psychobiology. [DNLM: 1. Aggression—
Congresses. W3 AD215 v. 12 / BF575.A3 W926n 1974]
BF575.A3N48   156'.24'2   74-23581
ISBN 0-306-37912-0

Proceedings of a conference held in
Newport Beach, California in March 1974

© 1974 Plenum Press, New York
A Division of Plenum Publishing Corporation
227 West 17th Street, New York, N.Y. 10011

United Kingdom edition published by Plenum Press, London
A Division of Plenum Publishing Company, Ltd.
4a Lower John Street, London W1R 3PD, England

Printed in the United States of America

Preface

This volume is based on papers presented at a Workshop on the
Neuropsychology of Aggression held at Newport Beach, California
in March 1974. The Workshop was sponsored by the Neuropsy-
chology Research Review Committee of the National Institute of
Mental Health (Grant #MH-23355-01) and by the Department of
Psychobiology of the University of California, Irvine.

The goal of the Workshop was to review contemporary approaches
to the study of aggression. Thus, the chapters of this book
cover not only conceptual issues, but also experimental techniques of genetic analysis, neuroanatomy, neurophysiology,
neuropharmacology and neuroendocrinology. It is hoped that
these chapters will be of value to investigators of the many
important problems of the nature of the biology of aggression.

Especial thanks go to Mrs. Chris Johnson who played a major
role both in organizing the Workshop and in preparing the
manuscripts for publication. In the latter task Miss Sue
McKenney also participated and deserves thanks.

Richard E. Whalen

Contents

Aggression and the Evolution of Man............... 1
    Ashley Montagu

Conceptual and Methodological Problems
Associated with the Study of Aggressive
Behavior in Primates under Seminatural
Conditions...................................... 33
    G. Gray Eaton

Experimental Analysis of Aggression and
its Neural Basis................................ 53
    John P. Flynn

Neurophysiological Approaches to the
Study of Aggression............................ 65
    Adrian A. Perachio and Margery Alexander

Behavioral Genetic Analyses of Aggression........ 87
    Gerald E. McClearn

Neuroanatomical Techniques for Neurobehavioral Research............................ 99
    Gary Lynch and Herbert Killackey

Physiological and Pharmacological
Analysis of Behavior........................... 125
    John A. Harvey

Hormone-Behavior Analysis........................ 149
    Richard E. Whalen

The Study of Human Aggression.................... 165
    John R. Lion and Manoel Penna

On Aggressive Behavior and Brain Disease -
Some Questions and Possible Relationships
Derived from the Study of Men and Monkeys.........   185
    Allan F. Mirsky and Nancy Harman

Participants.....................................   211

Index..   213

AGGRESSION AND THE EVOLUTION OF MAN

Ashley Montagu

Princeton, New Jersey 08540

Aggression and the Anthropological Evidence

Throughout their writings, innate aggressionists make it a
basic tenet of their argument that the evolution of man was
literally dependent upon the development of his aggressiveness. For example, in <u>On Aggression</u> Konrad Lorenz writes,
"When man, by virtue of his weapons and other tools, of his
clothing and fire, had more or less mastered the inimical
forces of his extra-specific environment, a state of affairs
must have prevailed in which the counter-pressures of the
hostile neighboring hordes had become the chief selecting
factor determining the next steps of human evolution. Small
wonder indeed if it produced a dangerous excess of what had
been termed the 'warrior virtues' of man" (p. 343).

These statements are typical of the amalgam of unsound
assumptions, alleged statements of fact, erroneous implications, and unwarranted inferences to be found in Lorenz's
book.

The attribution of weaponry to early man is pure assumption,
and is meant to imply that he employed weapons in hostile
conflict with other men. For this there is not one iota
of evidence. There is no evidence whatever that early man
made implements to serve as weapons. As for fire, that is

1

a late development in the evolution of man, dating back to
Peking Man some 600,000 years before the present, and like
clothing is hardly relevant to any consideration of the so-
called inimical forces of his extra-specific environment. We
assume that among these inimical forces were the alleged
"hostile neighboring hordes."

But there were no hostile neighboring hordes. There were
none for the simple reason that food-gathering hunting
populations are always very small in number, scarcely ever
exceeding more than a few families living together, such as
we find among the Eskimo, who until recently were exclusively
gatherer-hunters, and neighboring Malayan groups, the Punan
of Borneo, the Pygmies of the Ituri Forest, the Hadza of
Tanzania, the Birhor of Southern India, the Bushman of the
Kalahari Desert, and the few remaining Australian aboriginal
populations. "Hordes" are the invention of nineteenth
century antiquarians and their modern counterparts.

As for the allegations of hostility between neighboring prehistoric populations, there is not the least evidence of
anything of the sort having existed. This by no means rules
out the possibility that such hostilities may occasionally
have occurred. If such hostilities did occur, it is
extremely unlikely that they were frequent. Neighboring
populations in prehistoric times would have been few and
far between, and when they met it is no more likely that
they greeted each other with hostility than do gatherer-
hunter peoples today.

Paul Shepard, Visiting Professor of Environmental Perception
at Dartmouth College, has summed up the facts most accurately. He writes, "Courtesy links bands of hunters. When they
meet, usually at the boundaries separating their respective
areas, they are peaceful and cordial. Because of the quasi-
territorial face-off and because the serious matter of mate
selection and marriage is frequently a part of these meet-
ings, they are highly charged affairs. Tensions are
buffered by fixed procedure, by more or less formal ceremony
and contests of skill and courage. These vary greatly,
allowing for all kinds of personal involvement and conflict
within the overriding rules conducive to harmony. The
meeting is cause for celebration, dancing, information,
exchange, companionship, courtship, and trade are carried

on . . . Unlike farmers, their population is not chronic-
ally underspaced. Since men are not by nature territorial,
hunters do not repel invading bands" (Shepard, 1973).

The recently discovered food-gathering Tasaday of Mindanao
in the Philippines numbering 27 individuals, of whom 13 are
children, speak most illuminatingly to this point[*]. Their
friendliness and utter lack of aggression have impressed
all who have met them. Discovered in July, 1971, Kenneth
MacLeish writes of the Tasaday as "perhaps the simplest of
living humans, and those closest to nature, are gentle and
affectionate . . . Our friends have given me a new measure
of man. If our ancient ancestors were like the Tasadays,
we come of far better stock than I had thought" (MacLeish,
1972).

And, indeed, all that we know of gatherer-hunter peoples is
that they very much more closely resemble the Tasaday in
their relations with their fellow men than does the dismal
picture of our ancient forebears fantasied by the innate
aggressionists.

The Tasaday were first discovered in 1966 by a hunter named
Dafal who came from a southern Philippine tribe. Between
1966 and June, 1971, in which latter year Dafal led an
official party, including anthropologists, to the Tasaday,
he had visited them ten times, and his contacts have never
been less than friendly. In a report on them John Nance, an
English visitor to the Tasaday, states that "Killing animals
for food was a barbarism unknown until the intrusion of a
hunter from another tribe--a neat negation of the anthropologists' theory of 'natural man' as an instinctive vicious
predator". "They are", he writes, "altogether a loving,
gentle people. They have no weapons, and no apparent
aggressive instincts" (Nance, 1972).

In defense of anthropologists it should be said that the
vast majority do not subscribe to the theory of "natural
man" as "an instinctive vicious predator." Indeed, the
majority of anthropologists thoroughly repudiate such an
imputation.

---

[*]Foodgathering-hunting populations are small because their
way of life can only support a small number of people.

Peggy Durdin, an American writer who spent several days among
the Tasaday, says, "Among the most quickly discernible traits
are their capacity for affection (and relaxed expression of
it) and their sense of humor. Adults and children do not
seem afraid of being openly loving. . . It is a pleasure
to watch Tasaday behavior towards people they like." "The
Tasaday live this partly communal life in very close quarters
year after year, as their ancestors told them to do, with
remarkable harmony. I found no one who had heard them
exchange harsh words or even speak sharply to the young.
In the face of something displeasing they seem to use the
tactic of evasion: They simply walk away" (Durdin, 1972).

What the innate aggressionists will make of the Tasaday,
with their ability to live without weapons and without
aggression, will be interesting to learn. But to return to
Lorenz and his fancied "counter-pressures" of "hostile
neighboring hordes" acting as "the chief selecting factor
determining the next steps of human evolution" producing
"the warrior virtues of man", this may be answered by
Professor Elman Service's summarizing conclusion in his book
The Hunters. "The birth-death ratio in hunting-gathering
societies is such that it would be rare for population
pressure to cause some part of the population to fight
others for territorial acquisition. Even if such a circumstance occurred it would not lead to much of a battle. The
stronger, more numerous, group would simply prevail,
probably even without a battle, if hunting rights or rights
to some gathering spot were demanded" (Service, 1966).

Indeed, there is no good reason why gatherer-hunter bands
should ever indulge in hostilities with neighboring bands,
since there are, in fact, no "counter-pressures" of any sort
involved, no material goods, no capital, territory, or other
valuables to plunder. Conflict between bands when, on
occasion, it does occur, is usually due to some kind of
unacceptable personal behavior, an elopement, gossip, an
affront, or the like. When the whole band is involved,
hostilities are of the most formalized kind, and seldom
last more than a few hours at most. As soon as the first
man is wounded, usually in a limb, hostilities are at an
end. Negotiations are then commenced in order to make
adequate reparation to the family of the injured man for
the pain and inconvenience that has been caused.

Where a strong sense of territory existed, as among the Ona of Tierra del Fuego and the Andaman Islanders in the Bay of Bengal, occasional conflict between bands would result in some bloodshed. But these are the exceptions among gatherer-hunter peoples. Killings among all these groups were and are rare.

So much, then, for Lorenz's and Ardrey's chimerical anthropology, which is typical not only of their writings, but stand also as examples illustrative of the manner in which most of the innate aggressionists deal, or rather do not deal, with the relevant evidence. It is a characteristic of such writers that they largely neglect to consider the evidence that the anthropological researches of the last fifty years have made available relating to the principal conditions that were operative in the evolution of man both as a physical and a behaving organism. This is, perhaps, not altogether surprising since in spite of the extended attention devoted by Darwin in The Descent of Man (1871) to the importance of social factors in the evolution of man, as well as by several subsequent writers, such as Henry Drummond (1894) and Carveth Read (1925) anthropologists themselves until recently failed to pay attention to that critical interconnection. Since that interconnection is fundamental for any real understanding of the nature of aggression in man, in what follows I shall attempt to set out its elements.

What virtually all writers on man's supposed innate propensity for aggression fail to understand is that man has experienced a unique evolutionary history--a history which has resulted in the development of a way of adapting himself to the challenges of the environment which is learned rather than biologically inherited. Man has, in fact, moved over into a completely new zone of adaptation, the man-made part of the environment, that part of the environment which has been invented and developed by man and socially transmitted from one generation to another. This learned part of the environment is what the anthropologist calls culture, man's adaptive dimension. Culture represents man's virtually exclusive means of meeting the challenges of the environment and both controlling and mastering it.

With some degree of security we can today reconstruct something of the manner in which our ancestors first commenced
the shift into this novel zone of adaptation.

The order of mammals to which man belongs in common with
about 150 other species, the primates, is, with the excep-
tion of the baboons and man, a forest-dwelling group.
Sometime in the Pliocene, about 10 million years ago, as a
consequence of climatic changes in Africa, extending from
the tip of South Africa to beyond the Equator, large areas
of this thickly forested continent underwent deforestation.
As a consequence of this gradual ecological change a large
number of animals, among them the ancestors of man, found
themselves expelled from this Garden of Eden onto open
plains, comparatively thinly vegetated and with few trees,
the so-called savanna. A savanna is, as it were, a cross
between a woodland and a desert.

Animals that live in forests tend to be plant-eaters. All
primates are predominantly vegetarian, supplementing their
diet occasionally with insects, eggs, birds, and sometimes
small animals. Chimpanzees will occasionally eat young
baboons, bushpigs, and bushbuck while baboons will kill and
eat mole-rats, gazelles, monkeys, bushbabies, antelopes,
and birds. But predominantly the primates are vegetarians.
Man still retains the long intestinal tract of a plant-
eater. From the remains of their meals we know that the
diet of the australopithecines, in addition to plant foods,
included slow-moving animals like frogs, catfish, turtles,
and the young of larger animals. The remains of such
meals have been found in association with the fossil remains
of Australopithecus boisei at Olduvai Gorge, Tanzania (East
Africa), dating back some 1.8 million years.

The next step from the gathering of slow-moving and juvenile
animals, we now conjecture, was the extension of this way
of life to the pursuit of their larger faster-moving
representatives, that is, to the invention of hunting.
Hunting is not an invention of man. It is something that
all carnivores do. Among primates, chimpanzees were thought
to hunt largely, as it were, by accident or serendipity, as
when they unexpectedly come upon an unanticipated meal and
then to pursue it either alone or in cooperation with other
chimpanzees (van Lawick-Goodall, 1971). It is, however,

now known that chimpanzees are skilled hunters who deliberately set out in search of prey in areas where they know
that animals they enjoy eating are likely to be found (Teleki,
1973). They will hunt only the juvenile animals and those
smaller than themselves, and leave the larger stronger more
dangerous ones strictly alone. This is where the hunting of
man and the hunting of chimpanzees differs. Man's mode of
hunting differed from that of chimpanzees in that he regarded
as his prey any other animal that could serve as food, no
matter what its size or strength. Early man's hunting of small
animals would not have required the invention of elaborate
implements. Such implements would have been developed only
much later when man commenced to hunt large animals. The
later invention of hunting devices, the digging of pits, the
setting of snares, the laying of traps, the making of tools
not merely to serve a specific domestic function but also
to serve a technological purpose, that is, the making of
other tools, brings us to the definition of man. The proper
definition of man is not simply that he is the toolmaking
animal, but that he is the animal that makes tools with
which to make other tools, a precedure upon which he becomes
dependent for his continued existence. There are other
animals that use use tools, and there are some, like the
orang that can improvise tools out of straw in a cage
(Montagu, 1930). The chimpanzee can make simple tools out
of such things as a twig with which to "fish" for termites,
and crude sponges are made by crushing leaves to take up
water for drinking or to wipe away dung or blood. No
animal, however, other than man manufactures tools with
which to make other tools, and no other animal is dependent
upon its toolmaking activities for its continued existence.

The hunting of large animals implies the development of a
high degree of intelligence, for not only have the appropriate implements to be invented with which to conduct the
hunt of animals so much larger and stronger, and in most
cases swifter, than the hunter, but it also implies planning,
cooperation, signaling, and communication over proximate and
not so proximate distances. All these skills did not spring
into being all at once from the cerebral hemispheres of
man's ancestors, but developed over many hundred of thousands
and, indeed, quite probably over several millions of years.

Beyond all other things hunting places the greatest premium
upon the problem-solving abilities of the hunters. Problem-
solving is the plain English for what we mean by intelligence, and intelligence is the ability to make the most
appropriately successful response to the particular challenge
of the situation. In pursuing his prey the hunter soon
discovers that he can best do so in cooperation with one or
more others. The pursued animal does not run in a straight
line, and often changes course, requiring rapid calculations
on the part of the hunters and quick changes in logistics
and strategies. It is vitally necessary, if the hunt is to
succeed, that these quick-changing strategies be communicated
to one's companions in the hunt. This may be done quietly
by signaling or by voice when running. I suspect that
language was invented under such hunting conditions, or if
it was not it was certainly elaborated under their influence
(Montagu, 1967).

In the new hunting way of life, especially of large swift-
moving animals, the male would, for the first time among
primates, begin to share food with the female and the
young, even though the greater part of the food upon which
the family subsisted was probably supplied by the foraging
of the females in the band. (Among contemporary gatherer-
hunters about 80 per cent of the food is brought in by the
women.) Those members who were most successful in the hunt
in maintaining an adequate food supply for their families
would clearly be most likely to contribute their genes to
succeeding generations, to the gene pool.

The development of the nuclear or biological family, that
is, mother, father, and children, the invention of large-
animal hunting, and all the associated inventions that
would result from such activities: the problem-solving, the
toolmaking and devising, the new means of communications,
shelter, transportation, social organization, and so on,
would require not only a large brain in which to store all
the accumulated information necessary for continued existence
in the human band, but an increasingly extended period of
infant dependency and childhood during which the young
member of the band could learn how to become a cooperative
and efficient contributor to its continued survival. The
long extended period of infant and childhood dependency
necessitates females who, as mothers, are efficiently able

to minister to the dependent needs of their young over a
considerable number of years, and of males who, as fathers
and husbands, are capable of the cooperative behavior
necessary for the healthy development of the nuclear family.
In brief, the highest selective premium is placed upon
having the greatest ability to love, love being defined
operationally as the ability to confer survival benefits
upon the other in a creatively enlarging manner. This means
that one behaves toward the other in a manner which not only
enables them to survive, but also to be more fully realized
in their potentialities for similar behavior than they would
otherwise have been. In males the highest selective premium
is placed upon the ability to cooperate, not alone with the
members of one's family, but with all the other members of
the group. In the small populations of prehistoric man,
which means during more than 99 per cent of man's evolutionary history, love and cooperation were vitally necessary and
indispensable forms of behavior between members of the band
if that band was to survive. It is the form of behavior
that most students of gatherer-hunter populations have
especially remarked, and it is especially evident among the
gatherer Tasaday of Mindanao.

Let us consider some other gatherer-hunter peoples, for
these peoples have lived and in many cases still live under
conditions very closely resembling those of our prehistoric
ancestors.

The aboriginal Tasmanians, for example, a people whom the
British managed to exterminate singlehandedly by 1873, were
a strikingly peaceful people. Robert Thirkell, who lived
among them for many years, "found them an inoffensive race
of people . . ." He never considered it necessary to carry
firearms to protect himself against them. Thirkell considered any injury sustained by the white settlers entirely
occasioned by their own ill-usage of the females (Thirkell,
1874; Roth, 1899). Even George Arthur, the lieutenant-
governor, appointed to drive them from their ancestral
hunting grounds, described the Tasmanians as "a noble-
minded race" (Turnbull, 1948). Nevertheless, the attempt
of the Tasmanians to defend themselves against their
oppressors met with the most brutal punishment, and within
75 years of the first fatal impact, total extermination.

The attempts of the Tasmanians to defend themselves against
the brutal whites, merely succeeded in getting themselves
denounced as "warlike" and their "noble" benefactors thought
of as the injured party. As the Reverend Thomas Atkins wrote
after visiting Tasmania in 1836, "Indeed, from a large induction of the facts, it seems to me to be a universal law in
the Divine government, when savage tribes who live by hunting
and fishing, and on the wild herbs, roots, and fruits of the
earth, come into collision with civilised races of men,
whose avocations are the depasturing of flocks and herds,
agricultural employments and commercial pursuits, the savage
tribes disappear before the progress of civilised races.
Indeed, they have not complied with the condition on which
'the Lord of the whole earth' granted to the first pro-
genitors of our race the habitable world. 'For God blessed
them, and God said unto them, be fruitful and multiply, and
replenish the earth and subdue it" (Turnbull, 1948).

The Reverend Thomas Atkins was speaking for millions of
white men then and later, and voiced the sentiments that
many more millions share with him across the length and
breadth of the Anglo-Saxon world. Today the doctrine is
called by its proper name: racism.

The Bushmen of South Africa have been somewhat romanticized.
They are not as gentle as many of us have been led to
believe, but nor are they as violent as some would have us
think. The Bushmen, who live on the edges of the Kalahari
Desert in Botswana and South-West Africa, occupy a land
which is anything but the flat, harsh, dry, hostile, forbidding country of thirst, heat, and thorns, of hunger and
death it has been painted. Water is a problem, but it is a
problem that is continually being solved. Food is, in fact,
abundant, and life is leisurely (Thomas, 1959; Lee, 1972).
Life is neither nasty, brutish, nor short. The Bushman
shares food with others, and repressing any feelings of
jealousy and possessiveness, he lives amicably enough with
his fellows and with his neighbors (Sahlins, 1972). Both
Professor Richard B. Lee and Professor Patricia Draper
found that the !Kung Bushmen deliberately choose not to live
in large groups in order to avoid the conflicts that frequently arise in such aggregations (Draper, 1973). The
human press among the !Kung Bushmen, with the average
density of thirty people in the camps at about one person
per 188 square feet (as compared with the 350 square feet

generally recognized as desirable) is notably not associated
with any recognizable symptoms of biological stress. This
may be due to the option the Bushmen enjoy of moving from
one band to another. Band fission of this type appears to
be a common technique among band-level peoples that they
employ to avoid conflict. Individual Bushmen are capable
of anger and even of losing their temper to the extent of
indulging in violence, but such occasions are comparatively
rare (Thomas, 1959). As a Bushman, witnessing such a loss
of temper remarked, "If you want to help people don't get
angry with them. Keep calm." Professor Draper writes me
that one of the mechanisms that works against violent con-
frontations between hostile individuals is the bickering
which is endemic to !Kung life. The !Kung neither brood nor
keep silent about interpersonal problems. They scold, com-
plain, make speeches, and so on. She thinks that this has
the effect of reducing tensions before they reach dangerous
levels. "It is also true", Dr. Draper writes me, "that
physical attack and domineering behavior are strongly
devalued by the culture and that these behaviors are rare
and not readily available for children and adolescents to
model themselves after. Overall, I would say that the
everyday potential for violent behavior is much lower
among the !Kung than it is for ourselves or for the neighboring Bantu peoples in the Kalahari" (Draper, personal
communication).

Dr. Draper, who made a special study of the matter, found
that !Kung parents do not physically punish children, and
that since aggressive postures are avoided by adults and
devalued by society at large, children have little opportunity to observe or imitate overtly aggressive behavior.
"Among the !Kung", she writes, "there is an extremely low
tolerance for aggressive behavior by anyone, male or female"
(Draper, 1974a). Competitiveness in games is almost
entirely lacking, and the players appear to come into a
game for the sheer joy of it and for practicing his own
skill at it (Draper, 1974b).

Quarrels occur, but like summer showers, they soon blow
over and serve to clear the air. No malice is borne, and
the deep involvement in each other is clearly exhibited
whenever any mischance or accident befalls a member of the
band. There is no aggressiveness toward other groups, no
raiding, no war. From past experience the Bushmen are

aware that white men are likely to be dangerous, and so
their tactic is to avoid them, to make themselves invisible
by concealment or flight. While each group has its own specific territory, which the group alone may use, they respect
the territories of others scrupulously, and there is no
fighting between neighbors.

When quarrels do break out between members of different
bands they are almost invariably on account of adultery.
Men may fight their wives, women may fight women, and men
other men. Wrestling to the ground may occur, and sexual
insults hurled at each other. If matters get heated enough
someone may shoot a poisoned arrow, with lethal effect. But
when this occurs hostilities cease and everyone joins in a
trance dance, a kind of ritual healing of wounds. Such
band quarreling is, however, rare.

The point to be emphasized here is that while intragroup
aggressiveness occurs among Bushmen, they avoid all intergroup friction. To use Lorenz's phrase, whatever "counter-
pressures of the hostile neighboring hordes" they might
possibly be exposed to, the Bushmen successfully avoid them
by simply making themselves scarce, and for a band of some
twenty or so individuals this is not difficult.

Professor Robin Fox of the Department of Anthropology of
Rutgers University tells us that "Pueblo Indians, Eskimos,
and Bushmen have all been cited as examples of non-violent
peoples, and all turn out to have high rates of personal
violence." He cites no evidence for this statement, except
to say that "The Bushmen have a higher homicide rate than
Chicago" (Fox, 1973). This is, of course, a piece of
statistical sleight of hand. When one compares rates for
any comparable trait of a population numbering about twenty
people with that of a city numbering some four million the
rates are going to be considerably higher in the tiny
population as compared with the larger. For example, if
one homicide a year occurred among the Bushmen the homicide
rate would still be much higher than the daily homicide rate
in Chicago. If there were one fractured limb a year among
Bushmen the annual Bushman fracture rate would exceed the
daily Chicagoan rate. Does this mean that Chicagoans are
less prone to bone breakage than Bushmen? It does not.

What it means is that as compared with Bushmen, Chicagoans
suffer a far greater number of fractures, but that these are
distributed over a much larger number of people. And so it
is with homicide. There are no daily homicides among
Bushmen, but there are among Chicagoans. Homicides are
infrequent among Bushmen. They are frequent among Chicagoans.

Professor Fox goes on to tell us that a book was written
about the Bushmen called The Harmless People, "which only
goes to show", he writes, "that while anthropologists might
be nice folks who like to think well of their fellow men,
they can be poor guides to reality."

Upon this it may be remarked that the book to which Professor
Fox refers was not written by an anthropologist, nor did
its author, Mrs. Elizabeth Marshall Thomas, bestow the name
upon the Bushmen which serves for the title of her book.
It is the name by which Mrs. Thomas thought the Bushmen
call themselves Zhu/wasi or zhu twa si, as Professor Fox
might have discovered had he read the first chapter of
Mrs. Thomas' book. In this instance, at least, Professor
Fox is not a good guide to reality.

Let us consider the facts more in detail. Dr. Richard B.
Lee, whose span of fieldwork among the !Kung Bushmen covered
the years 1963-69, recorded 33 case histories in which
people came to blows. For the period 1920-69 Lee obtained
information on 15 major fights in which 22 people were
killed, the last fatal fight occurring in 1955. These
figures are derived from a total base population of 1300
!Kung Bushmen living in flexible social groupings of from
10 to 50 individuals.

Lee found that a bystander or third party is more likely to
get killed in a Bushman fight than a principal in an
argument. There is a general unpredictability about who
gets killed, and Lee suggests that Bushman fighting may
perhaps best be considered as a running amuck or temporary
insanity, rather than as an instrumental means-end behavior.

In fifty years Bushmen homicides totaled 22, which would
work out at a rate of 34 per 100,000 people. If one compares this with the U. S. homicide rate, and takes into

consideration the fact that in the United States many
people recover from attempts on their lives owing to
superior medical care, that large numbers of attempted
homicides go unreported, or are attributed to other causes,
that many deliberate homicides are caused by means that are
never recognized, to which one may add deaths caused by
American intervention in the affairs of foreign nations, then
the comparable American homicide rate rises to about 100 per
100,000 of the population.

All observers of the Bushmen are agreed that the fear of
violence is a prominent feature of their life. Hence,
nothing came as a greater relief to them than the setting up
of a headman's court in 1948, a court to which they could
bring their serious conflicts for adjudication. Homicides
occurred in 1952 and 1955, but none have occurred since
then.

The point here is not that the Bushmen are nonviolent, but
that while they are capable of violence they fear its
consequences and have taken full advantage of the opportuni-
ties provided them to control any violent impulses they
might experience, preferring to have their serious conflicts
resolved peacefully. Far from surpassing Chicago in its
homicide rates, the Bushmen were and are rarely homicidal.
As Lee says, the balance sheet distinctly favors the
savage who, even in the absence of other superordinate means
of social control manages to keep his violence rate low, so
that for all their poisoned arrows the !Kung Bushmen may be
"the harmless people" after all (Lee, 1969).

The Eskimos are perhaps the most written about gatherer-
hunter people of all. Everyone who has lived among Eskimos
and has written about them has always done so with unfailing
admiration and enthusiasm. Living, as they do, in the most
inhospitable lands in the world, in icy wastelands in which
during the dark winter nights the temperature falls to 50
and 60 degrees below zero, where there is virtually a
complete absence of any form of vegetation; above the ice
seeking for fish or seal for hours without moving, or being
tossed about in a tiny skin boat on a stormy sea in search
of the food it may supply, subject to the severest tests
to which anyone can be put, the Eskimo is perhaps best

described in the words of Admiral Peary. Writing of the
Eskimos of West Greenland, he says, "They are savages, but
they are not savage; they are without government, but they
are not lawless; they are utterly uneducated according to our
standard, yet they exhibit a remarkable degree of intelligence.
In temperment like children, with all a child's delight in
little things, they are nevertheless endearing as the most
mature of civilized men and women, and the best of them are
faithful unto death. Without religion and having no idea of
God, they will share their last meal with anyone who is
hungry, while the aged and the helpless among them are taken
care of as a matter of course. They are healthy and pure-
blooded; they have no vices, no intoxicants, and no bad habits--
not even gambling. Altogether they are a people unique upon the
face of the earth. A friend of mine calls them the philosophic
anarchists of the north . . . To Christianize them would be
quite impossible; but the cardinal graces of faith, hope, and
charity they seem to have already, for without them they would
 never survive the six-months' night and the many rigors of
their home" (Peary, 1910).

No one, in so few words, has better characterized the Eskimo.
In his classic book on these peoples Kaj Birket-Smith
describes them as individualists who consider nothing "more
repulsive than aggressiveness and violence", and he makes
the point that "far-reaching helpfulness among camp-fellows
is an inevitable duty" (Birket-Smith, 1959).

For every Eskimo tribal group and band the story is the same.
In the latest book by an anthropologist on an Eskimo family
(Briggs, 1970) with whom she lived, Jean Briggs tells us how
the Utku of the Back River, northwest of Hudson Bay, would,
early in their relationship, have nothing to do with her
because she lost her temper with some visiting fishermen who
carelessly broke one of the Eskimo's canoes. This unseemly
and frightening display of wrath, even though it was aimed
against uninvited intruders who had irresponsibly damaged
one of their most prized possessions, caused her to be
ostracized for some three months. Stinginess, unhelpfulness,
and bad temper are three of the most damning traits in the
Utkus' view that could be ascribed to anyone.

Nevertheless, some people do occasionally become angry, and quarrels occur between individuals, between bands, and with other tribes, but these seldom result in violence of any kind, although murder is not unknown, but again, it is rare. The traditional manner of settling disputes is by the contestants "assaulting" each other with reproachful songs. This is done to a musical accompaniment and is a source of great delight to those present. It is a form of "aggression" from which the civilized world could greatly benefit were it possible to persuade it to adopt this engaging convention.

Among the East Greenland Eskimos, for example, the song-contest is the customary means of settling a dispute or grudge. Even the murder of a relative may be settled in this way, especially if the relative seeking satisfaction feels himself so skilled in singing that he is sure of victory. Since skill in singing is greatly admired and the artistry of the performer so absorbs the interest of the audience, the cause of the contest tends to be forgotten, and the focus of attention is entirely upon the wit and skill with which the contestants attempt to outsing each other. He who delights the audience most and receives the heartiest applause is declared the winner. Singing skill, indeed, equals or outranks gross physical prowess and brings great prestige (Hoebel, 1954).

As human beings the Eskimos are capable of the full range of human emotions and behavior, and their choice is to be gentle cooperative people who place a high value on loving and being loved; as such, they pursue a wholly unaggressive way of life.

The Pygmies of the Ituri Forest of Central Africa, live in a world that for them is good, living as they do within the warm embrace of the forest in peace and amity with all about them. The Mambuti, as they call themselves, average less than four and a half feet in height, but what they lack in height they make up for in strength and toughness.

Colin Turnbull, who lived among the Pygmies for three years, says of them, "Cooperation is the key to Pygmy society; you can expect it and you can demand it, and you have to give it. If your wife nags at you at night so that you cannot

sleep, you merely have to raise your voice and call on
your friends and relatives to help you. Your wife will do
the same, so whether you like it or not the whole camp
becomes involved" (Turnbull, 1969). Anger may arise,
quarrels may start, children may be slapped for doing something wrong, but anger does not last long, grudges are not
borne, quarrels are evanescent, and occasional chastisement
of one's wife or husband is as far as any form of violence
goes. The Pygmies are unaggressive both emotionally and
physically, as is evidenced by their lack of any form of
warfare, feuding, witchcraft, and sorcery (Turnbull, 1968).
Turnbull believes that the kind of quarreling, spouse-beating,
and other similar activities that go on within the anything
but quiet Pygmy camp, constitute outlets which, together
with the explicit concern for the avoidance of aggression,
are designed to provide "insurance policies" against
aggression of an intended, calculated type.

At the time of their discovery in the late eighteenth
century there were several hundred tribes of Australian
aborigines, and what we know of them from early records and
later field studies it is clear that they were, and such of
them as remain are, to this day a highly cooperative and
unaggressive group of peoples. As W. E. Harney, who lived
the greater part of his life among the aborigines of Arnhem
Land, Northern Territory, has said, "Did you ever see a
native fight? All day it will go on, with plenty of running
about and talk and natives scruffing one another, but very
little bloodshed. Although they throw spears and boomerangs
about, it is very rarely that a person is seriously injured.
Of course, we think it silly. Understand, however, their
kinship rules, and you will notice that the talkers are the
protectors, whereas the actual combatants are kept away
from each other. Knowing this, the latter will roar and
shout and try to break away: but they are never let go until
their tempers have cooled off. Implicit in this behaviour
is the wise principle of 'Arbitration'" (Harney, 1943).

Of the Pitjantjatjaras of Ernabella in Central Australia,
to call upon yet another representative example, Hilliard
writes that they fight ceremonially, following the rule of
turn and turn about. In fights between women and those
between men "the fight clears the air and there are no grudges.
Once their quarrel has been settled, the ex-combatants
assist each other to receive first aid!" (Hilliard, 1968).

Warfare, defined as armed conflict carried on by members of
one social unit against another, and feuds, defined as
conflict between particular families or groups of kin,
did sometimes occur among the Australian aborigines.
Usually the conflicts were over a woman or a death believed
to have been caused by sorcery practiced by a member of
another band or tribe. Typically, as Spencer and Gillen
described the scene, the attackers entered their opponents'
camp fully armed, but fought with words, not weapons; after
a time things would quiet down, and the affair subsided.
Occasionally, however, they would come to blows, or the
avenging party would wait in hiding to spear their victim
or spear him after he had been ceremonially handed over by
his own group (Spencer and Gillen, 1927).

As our leading students of the Australian aborigines,
Professors A. P. Elkin of the Department of Anthropology at
the University of Sydney and Ronald Berndt and Catherine
Berndt at the University of Western Australia at Perth have
emphasized, territory is important to the aborigines neither
politically nor economically (Elkin, 1964; Berndt and Berndt,
1964). The tribe as a whole seldom, if ever, makes war.
This is a concern of local groups or clans. There are no
wars for territorial aggrandizement. War was, in fact, as
G. C. Wheeler showed many years ago, infrequent in aboriginal Australia (Wheeler, 1910).

In fact, students of the Australian aborigines all agree
that they are a particularly gentle, generous, kind, and
noble-hearted people (Lefroy, 1919). On occasion the
aborigines were capable of carrying out a sanctioned killing
in much the same manner in which a state-appointed execu-
tioner executes a condemned felon. Such killing, however,
partook more of the nature of a retributive exaction of a
penalty than it did of an aggressive act. As Buss has
pointed out, injurious attacks upon others may not be
considered aggressive if they occur within the context of
a socially accepted custom or role (Buss, 1961).

The two dozen or more gatherer-hunter peoples, in addition
to those I have already described, however they may vary
culturally, nevertheless preserve much the same general
tendencies toward aggressiveness, with the possible excep-
tion, as noted earlier, of the Ona of Tierra del Fuego and

the Andaman Islanders. There was much quarreling and
feuding within the band among the Yaghans and between bands
among the Ona, usually over the theft of a woman or because
of trespass. Unlike the other peoples I have described
the Ona bands, of which there were some thirty-nine, each
had a leader, whose authority was especially evident when
conflict of any kind threatened or occurred. Furthermore,
since the Ona forbade marriage of both maternal and
paternal cousins, they had no ambassadors, as it were, in
other bands since interband cousin marriage was forbidden.
These two facts, the emergence of a band leader and the
prohibition of cousin marriage, constitute part of a
political situation which, as Coon puts it, "marks a trans-
ition between a bilateral, loosely organized system which
lacked firm authority to a unilateral one in which leader-
ship was more nearly crystallized. It also marks a change
from disorganized brawls and fights starting with individuals to concerted raids and ordeals between groups" (Coon,
1971).

The Andaman Islanders, who live on the islands in the Bay
of Bengal off the tip of the coast of Southern India, are
pygmies, who also had band leaders or chiefs exercising
power over them, one for the coastal bands and one for the
inland bands. Killings within a band were rare, but were
more frequent between bands. By 1911 superior band chiefs
had disappeared, and the population was so reduced that
there were no longer a sufficient number of bands left
to indulge in the luxuries of feuding and fighting.

Radcliffe-Brown states that fighting on a large scale seems
to have been unknown among the Andamanese, and that their
only fights among themselves were brief and far from bloody,
where only a handful of men were engaged on each side and
rarely more than one or two killed. "Of such a thing as
war in which the whole of the tribe joined to fight with
another tribe" Radcliffe-Brown could find no evidence (Radcliffe-Brown, 1933).

Even though in most ways the gatherer-hunter peoples I have
described may be socially more advanced than were our prehistoric gatherer-hunter ancestors, their ways of life are
much closer to those of our ancestors than to ours, and
tell us a great deal more about the ways of life of our

prehistoric ancestors. What the gatherer-hunter peoples
tell us is that although, on occasion, prehistoric men were
capable of aggressive behavior, they most certainly, for
the most part, led peaceful lives, that they must have been
highly cooperative and deeply involved in the welfare of
their fellow man.

If any people stands closest to our prehistoric ancestors
it may well be the food-gathering Tasaday of Mindanao,
undoubtedly among the gentlest and most unaggressive people
on this earth. What can have happened to that resevoir of
aggressiveness with which writers like Lorenz and Ardrey
would have us suppose that all human beings are endowed?
Can it be that they have learned to control the expression
of aggression? Or is it possible they may have lost the
genes associated with the potentialities for aggression?
Or is it that since they have no weapons they have never
developed "killer genes?" The probability of gene loss is
low. Control of aggression is a very much more likely
possibility, and an even more likely explanation is that
from infancy the Tasaday has learned to be cooperative and
unaggressive so that seldom, if at all, has a Tasaday been
called upon to harness any tendency toward aggression. One
learns to be unaggressive simply by not being aggressive
(Scott, 1958).

Learning is the increase in the strength of any act through
repetition in response to a task-situation induced directly
by experience. One can learn to be unaggressive just as
easily as one can learn to be aggressive. There is no
ineluctable necessity about aggression. It is not something that must inevitably develop and mature. Humans are
no more wired for aggression than they are for organized
homicide.

Control of aggression is clearly exercised by many peoples.
Indeed, aggression is controlled by individuals in most
societies. But that is a very different phenomenon from
the behavior presented by the Tasaday, who may have no
aggression because they have never learned to behave
aggressively. This is not to suggest that they lack the
biologic potentialities for behaving aggressively, but it
is to suggest that in the Tasaday world those potentialities
have not received those organizing stimulations necessary
for the development of aggressive behavior. What seems to
me most likely is a combination of this explanation with the

theory of control, namely, that the Tasaday have both
learned to be cooperative and unaggressive and have also
learned to control such feelings of aggression or aggressivity they may on occasion experience. These occasions
are likely to be few, first because they have been trained
in cooperation, second because they have been trained out of
any tendencies toward aggression, and third because they are
seldom exposed to conditions that would be productive of
aggression.

Why are gatherer-hunter peoples on the whole characterized
by so little aggression? Can it be that they have so little
to be aggressive about? Can it be that while man lives in
small groups in precarious relation to his environment, that
he must be a cooperator, that any undue aggressiveness might
fatally upset the delicate balance which the small group must
preserve if it is to maintain itself? (cf. Turnbull, 1972).

I think it not only can be, but that it is highly probable
that in the course of man's evolution as a gatherer-hunter
the highest premium was placed by natural selection on
cooperative behavior, and a negative premium on aggressive
traits.

It is difficult to conceive of any useful function aggression
would have played either between members of the prehistoric
band or between bands in the sparsely populated regions of
the earth in which man lived. Indeed, as J. B. S. Haldane
pointed out in his book The Causes of Evolution (1932), "In
so far as it makes for the survival of one's descendants and
near relations, altruistic behaviour is a kind of Darwinian
fitness, and may be expected to spread as a result of
natural selection" (Haldane, 1932).

It could, of course, be argued that once such fitness had
been established within the group, that fitness could be
further enhanced by trial by combat, in which the worthiness
of the one or the other group to survive and bequeath its
genes to succeeding generations could be tested. This has
indeed been argued by Dr. Robert Bigelow in a book entitled
The Dawn Warriors (1969). Bigelow suggests that man evolved
both as an intragroup cooperator and an intergroup aggressor,
whose most deadly enemies were human foreigners. "The survival of our species", he urges, "now, depends on our
ability to suppress the urge to kill our enemies."

The facts, however, do not support such arguments and claims.
The record of history bears vivid testimony to the fact that
virtually everywhere when nonliterate peoples encountered
the white man for the first time they welcomed him with
every token of friendship. If some of these peoples were in
conflict with neighboring bands or other groups, it was
certainly not because they were foreigners, but because
of some grievance, fancied or real; not because they were
driven by some "urge to kill" their enemies, but because
from past experience they had learned that some form of
aggressive behavior was the appropriate means of dealing with
the situation. Some peoples have learned that the appropriate response is with nonaggressive behavior. It depends
upon the culture and its particular history (Mead, 1937).
Aggression occurs only in cultures in which the individual
is conditioned in aggressive behavior.

Among peoples practicing some form of agriculture such as
the Papago Indians, the Hopi, the Zuni, and the Pueblo
peoples generally, any form of aggressive behavior is
thoroughly condemned. So, too, it is disapproved among the
Semai of Malaya and neighboring tribes. The Punan of Borneo
(Hose, 1926), the Land Dayaks of Sarawak (Geddes, 1961), the
Polynesian Tikopia of the Western Pacific (Firth, 1957) who,
even under conditions of famine and considerable social
change preferred to express their anger in words rather than
in physical violence (Firth, 1959). The Lepchas of Sikkim
in the Himalayas, a nomadic pastoral people, are most gentle
and unaggressive, living at peace with their neighbors and
with themselves in spite of a life that is hard and continuously trying (Gorer, 1938). The Polynesian Ifaluk of the
Western Pacific are another such gentle people, although
life for them is much easier than it is for the Lepchas.
Marston Bates describes the Ifaluk as the "most completely
non-aggressive society imaginable" (Bates, 1953). On their
small coral atoll the Ifaluk have enjoyed the greatest
freedom from contact with civilized people of any of the
Pacific Islanders. Kindliness, security, and serenity are
the outstanding traits of the Ifaluk personality (Bates and
Abbott, 1958). Every child was a member not only of a
family and a household, but of the whole island society. A
child crying would be comforted by the nearest adult."
"Curiously," adds Bates, "the children, though 'secure,'
were far from obnoxious--in fact it would be difficult to

imagine a more delightful bunch of kids. The 'sibling
rivalry' that seems to plague every American household was
conspicuous by its absence--the mannerly, non-aggressive
character of Ifaluk society extended even to the five-year-
olds."

The remarkable Tarahumara Indians of Mexico, who can run a
hundred miles or more at an average speed of 6 to 7 miles
per hour without resting, are equally remarkable for their
dignity, respect for others, good humor among themselves, and
helpfulness toward strangers. Intergroup or intragroup
violence is unknown. In the past quarter of a century
there have been no suicides and only one homicide among the
50,000 tribesmen. Dr. Louis J. West and Dr. Clyde C. Snow of
the University of California at Los Angeles, comment that
the often great and forbidding distances between individual
families "undoubtedly cause people to be keenly aware of
their need for each other and appreciative of the value of
persons" (West, Paredes, and Snow, 1969; Bennet and Zingg,
1936; Cassel, 1969). And all this under the most bleak and
trying conditions, where hunger and disease are the daily
experience of all.

Space forbids the discussion of the numerous other peaceful
peoples, like those of Tibet (Bell, 1928), the Subarctic
(Levin and Potapov, 1964), the Lapps (Bosi, 1960), the
peoples of Malaya (Skeat and Blagden, 1966; Winstedt, 1950),
and other, such as the Arapesh of the Sepik River in New
Guinea, so well described by Margaret Mead in Sex and
Temperament in Three Primitive Societies (1935).

Perhaps one of the most instructive case histories in the
matter of human aggression is afforded by the story of the
Pitcairn Islanders. Almost everyone now knows of the
famous mutiny on the Bounty in 1789, the English naval
vessel commanded by Captain Bligh, and the escape of nine
of the mutinous seamen together with six Tahitian men and
twelve Tahitian women to Pitcairn Island. Of the fifteen
men who landed on Pitcairn in 1789, ten years later there
were only two left. All of the Tahitian men and four of
the Englishmen having fallen victim to the weapons of their
fellow settlers. Even the women had participated in some
of the murders and had planned others. From such an
unpromising beginning one would have expected a continuingly

violent society. But the unexpected happened. From 1799 to
the present day there has been only one crime of violence,
a murder in 1895 of his wife and child, by a Pitcairn
Islander. The only serious offence that has occurred since
is wifebeating. Dr. Harry Shapiro, who visited Pitcairn in
December, 1934, commented on the rarity of disputes and
disagreements. "The community", he wrote, "by universal
testimony of its visitors, was remarkably harmonious and
cooperative" (Shapiro, 1936). Walter Brodie, who visited the
island in 1850, remarked, "Quarrels and swearing were unknown
among the islanders" (Brodie, 1851). And this in a population which averaged well over one hundred individuals.
In 1972, when the population stood at 89, Ian M. Ball, a
New Zealand journalist, and his family could, after a
diligent inquiry, find no evidence of aggressive behavior.
Ball came to the conclusion that "wrongdoing on Pitcairn
Island is limited very largely to two categories--wifebeating
and juvenile mischief" (Ball, 1973). No one within living
memory could recall the single-room jail's having been
occupied, a fact to which the rusted hinges on the
uncloseable door offered eloquent testimony. One cannot
help wondering what may have happened to the "spontaneity
of aggression" in the Pitcairn Islanders.

But we must bring this essay to a close. It is hoped that
it has been sufficiently shown that there are many peoples
of different kinds who are virtually completely unaggressive. Whether by trained control or otherwise, such
nonaggressive behavior is clearly learned, just as the
habit of being aggressive is learned in cultures in which
it is the habit to be aggressive. In such societies the
biological potentialities for aggression are socially
reinforced by the kinds of experiences which are permitted
in them. In either case, in societies in which aggression
is permitted and those in which it does not occur, learning
plays a dominant role, to such an extent in nonaggressive
societies, that the biological potentialities are simply
inhibited from developing.

It is well known from experimental studies that by doing
nothing or remaining passive, under the same conditions
which in others has by training evoked aggressive responses,
that the animal will learn to do nothing and remain passive.
This is known as passive inhibition and is undoubtedly the
means by which our peaceful peoples have learned to be
unaggressive (Scott, 1958).

In conclusion it should be said that the evidence considered
in this essay strongly tends to confirm the high probability
that man developed as a highly cooperative creature. It
further seems highly probable that aggressive behavior has
not been genetically built into him as an "urge to kill his
neighbors", but that, on the contrary, what has probably been
genetically built into him is an urge to cooperate with his
neighbors. Potentialities for aggressive behavior exist
within the brain of <u>Homo</u> <u>sapiens</u>, but in order to be
expressed in overt behavior they must be appropriately
stimulated by the cultural environment. And the same, of
course, holds true for cooperative behavior.

References

Ardrey, R. <u>African Genesis</u>. New York: Athenium, 1961.

Ball, I.M. <u>Pitcairn: Children of Mutiny</u>. Boston: Little,
        Brown & Co., 1973.

Bates, M. and Abbott, D. <u>Coral Island</u>. New York: Scribner's
        & Sons, 1958.

Bell, C. <u>The People of Tibet</u>. Oxford: Clarendon Press,
        1928.

Bennett, W.C. and Zingg, R.M. <u>The Tarahumara</u>. San Antonio:
        Taylor Co., 1969.

Berndt, R.M. and Berndt, C.H. <u>The World of the First
        Australians</u>. Chicago: University of Chicago Press,
        1964.

Bigelow, R. <u>The Dawn Warriors</u>. Boston: Little, Brown & Co.,
        1969.

Birket-Smith, K. <u>The Eskimos</u>. New York: Dutton, 1959.

Bosi, R. <u>The Lapps</u>. New York: Praeger, 1960.

Briggs, J.L. <u>Never in Anger</u>. Cambridge: Harvard University
        Press, 1970.

Brodie, W. Pitcairn's Island and Other Islanders in 1850.
        London: Whittaker & Co., 1851.

Buss, A.H. The Psychology of Aggression. New York: Wiley,
        1961.

Cassell, J.W. Tarahumara Indians. San Antonio: Taylor Co.,
        1969.

Coon, C.S. The Hunting Peoples. Boston: Little, Brown &
        Co., 1971.

Draper, P. Crowding among hunter-gatherers: The !Kung Bush-
        men. Science, 1973, 182, 301-303.

Draper, P. [a] !Kung women: Contrasts in sexual egalitarian-
        ism in the foraging and sedentary contexts. In
        Toward an Anthropology of Women, (R. Reiter, Ed.).

Draper, P. [b] Social and economic constraints on !Kung child-
        hood. In Kalahari Hunter Gatherers, (R.B. Lee and I.
        Devore, Eds.). Cambridge: Harvard University Press,
        1974.

Drummond, H. The Ascent of Man. London: Hodder & Stoughton,
        1894.

Durdin, P. From the space age to the Tasaday age. New York
        Times Magazine, 1972, Oct. 8.

Elkin, A.P. The Australian Aborigines. New York: Anchor
        Books, 1964.

Firth, R. We, the Tikopia. London: Allen & Unwin, 1957.

Firth, R. Social Change in Tikopia. New York: Macmillan,
        1959.

Fox, R. Encounter with Anthropology. New York: Harcourt,
        Brace & Jovanovitch, 1973.

Geddes, W.R. Nine Dyak Nights. New York: Oxford University
        Press, 1961.

Gorer, G. _Himalayan Village_. London: M. Joseph, 1938.

Haldane, J.B.S. _The Causes of Evolution_. London: Longmans,
        Green & Co., 1932.

Harney, W.E. _Taboo_. Sydney: Australian Publishing Co., 1943.

Hilliard, W. _The People in Betweeen_. New York: Funk &
        Wagnalls, 1968.

Hoebel, E.A. _The Law of Primitive Man_. Cambridge: Harvard
        University Press, 1954.

Hose, C. _Natural Man: A Record from Borneo_. London:
        Macmillan, 1926.

Lee, R.B. What hunters do for a living or how to make out
        on scarce resources. In _Man the Hunter_ (R.B. Lee and
        I. Devore, Eds.). Chicago: Aldine, 1968.

Lee R.B. !Kung Bushmen violence. Paper presented at the
        annual meeting of the American Anthropological Associa-
        tion, New Orleans, 1969.

Lee, R.B. The intensification of social life among the !Kung
        Bushmen. In _Population Growth: Anthropological Impli-
        cations_ (B. Spooner, Ed.). Cambridge: MIT Press, 1972.

Lefroy, C.E.C. Australian aborigines, a noble-hearted race.
        Contemporary Review (London), 1919, _135_, 222-223.

Levin, M.G. and Potapov, L.P. _The Peoples of Siberia_.
        Chicago: University of Chicago Press, 1964.

Lorenz, K. _On Aggression_. London: Metheden & Co., 1963.

MacLeish, K. Stone age cave men of Mindanao. _National
        Geographic_, 1972, August.

Mead, M. _Sex and Temperament in Three Primitive Societies_.
        New York: W. Morrow & Co., 1935.

Mead, M. _Cooperation and Competition Among Primitive People_.
        New York: McGraw-Hill, 1937.

Montagu, A. A note on the behavior of an Orang-Outan. J. Mammol., 1930, 11, 231-232.

Montagu, A. The Human Revolution. New York: Bantam Books, 1967.

Nance, J. The inheritors. Sunday Times Magazine (London), 1972, October 8.

Peary, R.E. To the North. New York: Doubleday, 1910.

Radcliff-Brown, A.R. The Andaman Islanders. Cambridge: Cambridge University Press, 1933.

Read, C. The Origin of Man. Cambridge: Cambridge University Press, 1925, 2nd ed.

Roth, L. The Aborigines of Tasmania. Halifax, England: F. King & Sons, 1899, 2nd ed.

Sahlins, M. Stone Age Economics. Chicago: Aldine-Atherton, 1972.

Scott, J.P. Aggression. Chicago: University of Chicago Press, 1958.

Service, E.R. The Hunters. Englewood Cliffs, N.J.: Prentice-Hall, 1966.

Shapiro, J.L. The Heritage of the Bounty. New York: Simon & Schuster, 1936.

Shepard, P. The Tender Carnivore and the Sacred Game. New York: Scribner's Sons, 1973.

Skeat, W.W. and Blagden, C.O. Pagan Races of the Malay Peninsula. New York: Barnes and Noble, 1966.

Spencer, B. and Gillen, F.J. The Arunta. New York: Macmillan, 1927, Vol. 1.

Teleki, G. The Predatory Behavior of Wild Chimpanzees. Lewisburg, Penna.: Bucknell University Press, 1973.

Thirkell, R. Notes on the aborigines of Tasmania. Proceedings of the Royal Society of Tasmania for 1873.

Thomas, E.M. The Harmless People. New York: Knopf, 1959.

Turnbull, Clive. The Black War. Melbourne: F.W. Cheshire, 1948.

Turnbull, Colin M. The Forest People. New York: Simon & Schuster, 1961.

Turnbull, Colin M. Discussion, in Man the Hunter (R.B. Lee and I. Devore, Eds.). Chicago: Aldine, 1968.

Turnbull, Colin M. The Mountain People. New York: Simon & Schuster, 1972.

van Lawick-Goodall, J. In the Shadow of Man. Boston: Houghton Mifflin, 1971.

West, L.J., Paredes, A. and Snow, C.C. A tribe that fascinates cardiology. Psychiatry, 1969, 208, 1617.

Wheeler, G.C. The Tribe and Intertribal Relations in Australia. London: J. Murray, 1910.

Winstedt, R. The Malays: A Cultural History. New York: Philosophical Library, 1950.

DISCUSSION

Smith: What sort of evidence do you feel would have to be forthcoming in order to show the innateness of aggressive behavior?

Montagu: I would want children to be raised in a humanizing environment, as they have been raised in food gathering-hunting peoples, and then to observe what happens to the spontaneous development of behavior that we could identify as aggressive.

Leshner: I am interested in knowing whether you think that some of our problems come from the definition of aggression.

Montagu: Yes. I think definition is very critical here. One of the characteristics of the innate aggressionists is that they use the word in an enormous variety of ways. When you finally boil down what they are getting at, they mean by aggression any behavior which is designed to inflict injury on another and that this is largely "wired."

Miczek: Do you think that hunting and predation have anything to say about fighting among species members?

Montagu: This is what the innate aggressionists say, namely that hunting behavior resulted in the invention of weapons which were then turned against other men. I am attempting to show that the evidence indicates quite the contrary. In the first place, weapons were not weapons, they were implements which were used for cutting up animals and obtaining tubers from the ground. If you examine these implements you see that the only way they could have been used as weapons would be to get the victim to lie down horizontally, immobile, then you would operate on him with a 2 1/2 inch pebble tool. They

30

could not have been used this way. To overcome
this difficulty, Professor Dart invented the
osteodontokeratic culture, a culture which
utilized horns, bones and teeth. You would have
a lower jaw that could be used as a saw and
portions of the scapula that you could break and
use as a dagger, a quite sophisticated implement
which was not invented until the Neolithic so
far as we know. My dealing with hunting is
designed to show that this was not a form of
behavior that was extended by early men to their
fellow human beings.

Potegal: Eibl-Eibesfeldt makes the claim that the former
description of the Bushmen is in error and that
indeed the homicide rate among Bushmen is
equivalent to that found in Houston. Is he
in error?

Montagu: Yes. He is quite right about the Kalahari being
romanticized. The two authorities who worked
with them in recent years are Patricia Draper
and Richard Lee. Their findings are clear. In
a retrospective study going back 50 years he
found 22 murders and for the size of the population this is a very large number, but this is
a statistical trick. If you compare a small
population with the population of Houston the
figures will give you a massive disproportion.
But they do not mean anything very significant.
If you study the Kalahari under conditions
where they have an agent to whom they can go to
resolve quarrels, there have been no violent
quarrels or murders since 1955 when this was
instituted.

Penna: How does one account for the great variability
in the expression of aggressive behavior within
the same culture?

Montagu: Largely, as a consequence of the conditioning
period, the socialization period. I would
assume on the basis of a great deal of evidence

from child growth and development studies that
a socialization period that has been a satisfying
one to the child is much more likely to result
in non-aggressive behavior while aggressive
behavior is likely to be the response to a
deprivation of love. I would say that a great
deal of human aggressive behavior is love
frustrated, a method of compelling attention to
one's need for love. This is what the work of
Bowlby, Golfarb and Spitz has shown.

CONCEPTUAL AND METHODOLOGICAL PROBLEMS ASSOCIATED WITH THE

STUDY OF AGGRESSIVE BEHAVIOR IN PRIMATES UNDER SEMINATURAL

CONDITIONS

G. Gray Eaton

Oregon Regional Primate Research Center

Beaverton, Oregon 97005

This paper is not a review of studies of primate aggressive behavior but an analysis of some of the problems involved in generating meaningful data under conditions of little control and an examination of the unique contribution such studies can make to the understanding of animal behavior. Primate aggressive behavior has been reviewed by Hall (1964), Washburn and Hamburg (1968), and Southwick (1972) and has received some attention in a review of primate communication by Peters and Ploog (1973). Aggressive behavior per se has been discussed by many authors including Collias (1944), Scott (1958), Carthy and Ebling (1964), and Rothballer (1967).

To study primate aggressive behavior in any environment, natural or seminatural, one needs to formulate a strategy, and such a strategy was provided by Beach (1960) in his discussion of investigating species-specific behavior.

"One merely attempts to answer three questions: How did the behavior get to be what it is? What are the

external causes of the behavior? What internal mechanisms mediate it? Phrased in slightly more sophisticated terms each of these questions can be said to
deal with a different class of determinants of behavior.
The determinants of behavior can be subdivided into
three broad categories: historical determinants, environmental determinants, and organismic determinants.

"In more familiar language, historical determinants are
in turn subdivisible into two classes which are usually
referred to as maturational and experiential factors.
Environmental determinants may be either direct or in-
direct .... The most frequently investigated organismic
determinants to date have been those of a neural or an
endocrinological nature." (Beach, 1960, p.5.)

In this paper, I discuss some methodological and conceptual
problems associated with establishing these determinants and
add some ideas from Schneirla (1950), Marler and Hamilton
(1966), Hinde (1970), and Altmann (1965; 1967) illustrating
them with examples from my own and others' research on primate
aggressive behavior in our Oregon troop of Japanese macaques.

Most, if not all, authors agree that the way to start is to
observe the animals. Herein lies one of the major advantages
of having a group of animals confined in a seminatural setting.
They can be studied intensively for long periods until obser-
vational techniques are perfected and the initial apparently
random and obscure patterns of behavior emerge in the observer's mind as acts that are significant in the social life of
the animals. Darling's (1937) frequently quoted statement
from his classic study of red deer bears repeating here because of the universality of this perceptual phenomenon and
its special importance to those who would study primate
behavior:

"It takes time for the eye to become accustomed to recognize differences, and once that has occurred the nature
of the differences has to be defined in the mind by careful self-interrogation if the matter is to be set down on
paper . . . . The fact remains that an observer has to
go through a period of conditioning of a most subtle
kind . . . .

The observer must empty his mind and be receptive only
of the deer and the signs of the country. This is quite
severe discipline, calling for time and practise ....
It is necessary intellectually to soak in the environmental complex of the animal to be studied until you have
a facility with it which keeps you as it were one move
ahead. You must become intimate with the animal ....
In this state the observer learns more than he realizes."
(Darling, 1937, p. 24-26).

In my experience with the Oregon troop of Japanese macaques,
all monkeys initially look alike; as a result, it takes months
of daily observations before a naive observer can accurately
identify just the adults in the troop by their faces and/or
physiques. After three years of daily observation, we cannot
yet accurately identify all the infants and juveniles; a few
of the adult females, however, can be recognized by their
voices. Symbols marked on the backs of juveniles and infants
with black dye (Anibrand Temporary Branding Dye, Acton
Associates, Pittston, Pa.) serve to identify them. Without
these marks, which last from early fall until the following
summer's moult, accurate identification would be impossible.
The ease of identifying every member of a troop quickly and
accurately is one of the advantages a seminatural situation
provides over a natural setting.

The next step is to objectively define the behavioral units
that are to be recorded. Two basic methods of behavioral
description (see Hinde, 1970) are currently used: the first
describes spatiotemporal patterns of muscle contractions,
the second describes behavioral actions by their consequence.
The latter method has several advantages which are especially
important in the study of primate aggressive behavior. A
brief description of behavioral actions by their consequences
includes a variety of motor patterns, e.g., one monkey can
attack another by biting or striking it. Such behavior can
be described in terms of objectively defined changes in the
environment. For example, in my own studies of aggressive
behavior in macaques, we differentiate between an "assault"
and a "punish" by defining them in terms of physical damage
to the attacked animal, i.e., blood is drawn or it is not.
Descriptions by consequence often call attention to aspects
of the behavior that may not appear in physical descriptions,
such as orientation to the environment or responsiveness to

external stimuli (Hinde, 1970). For example, the muscle
patterns of playful wrestling and biting are similar to those
of aggressive grappling and biting and can be distinguished
only by their intensity and the fact that the consequences
are quite different.

A decision must be subsequently made as to which behaviors are
to be described and which aspects of them are to be emphasized.
Marler stresses the importance of the initial selection of the
aspects of the situation that are to be recorded.

"If initial selection is so critical, the investigator
who tries to approach a project with a completely open
mind is less likely to be successful than one who attempts
to formulate the questions he wishes to answer. Yet it
is the very nature of progress to discover new questions
in the process of answering old ones. So the framework
of investigation should be flexible enough to allow
detection of the unforeseen yet rigid enough to insure
adequate preappraisal." (Marler and Hamilton, 1966,
p. 712).

Some time and effort can be saved if others have described
the behavior of the species of interest. Sade (1967), for
example, gave detailed descriptions of attack and flight
gestures in rhesus monkeys (Macaca mulatta) and concluded
that they agreed with those of Altmann (1962), Chance (1956),
Hinde and Rowell (1962), Rowell (1962), and Rowell and Hinde
(1962). A pitfall, however, awaits the neophyte primatologist
who neglects the conditioning described by Darling and blindly
accepts another's descriptions of behavior. Free-ranging
Japanese macaques (Macaca fuscata) have and use the ability
for socially acquiring signs (Stephenson, 1973). Males of
different troops courted females with different patterns of
behavior, and females mounted only high-ranking males in one
troop, only low-ranking males in another troop, and did not
mount any males in a third troop. This ability to use
arbitrary signs is probably shared by many other primate
species; whereas Stephenson observed group-specific signals
only in the context of courtship, they may well occur in
threat patterns which signal incipient attack.

Another problem associated with behavioral description
is the separation of sequences.

"Like other problems in classification, categorizing the
units of social behaviour involves two major problems:
when to split and when to lump. If one's goal is to draw
up an exclusive and exhaustive classification of the
animals' repertoire of socially significant behaviour
patterns, then these units of behaviour are not arbi-
trarily chosen. To the contrary, they can be empirically
determined. One divides up the continuum of action wherever
the animals do. If the resulting recombination units are
themselves communicative, that is, if they affect the
behaviour of other members of the social group, then they
are social messages. Thus, the splitting and lumping
that one does is, ideally, a reflection of the splitting
and lumping that the animals do." (Altmann, 1965, p. 492).

The observer's task is therefore to recognize "the criteria of
sequential demarcation" (Altmann, 1967) and then to formulate
the behavioral descriptions so that they can be reliably
quantified and empirically tested by other workers.

Categorical separations of behavioral units are of equal
importance. Although most of these have apparent face validity,
conceptual problems may arise that can be overcome only through
prolonged and careful observation.

"The biological criterion of natural classification is
that the fundamental classifications be based upon the
demarcations, both sequential and categorical, that occur
in the natural habitat of the species. This is not to
say that evidence for the natural classification cannot
be obtained from animals in laboratories, outdoor enclo-
sures, zoos, island colonies, and so forth. On the
contrary, for certain purposes such artificial colonies
often have definite advantages over natural habitats and
are highly recommended in preparation for any field study.
But the naturalness of a classification obtained under
such conditions is to be judged by the extent to which it
reflects what happens in the animals' natural habitat."
(Altmann, 1967, p. 357).

Carpenter (1942), for example, noted that rhesus females were
attacked by the males during the breeding season. The adult
males in the Oregon troop of Japanese macaques also threaten
and attack females during the breeding season. Their threats,

however, are similar to some patterns of courtship and were
confused by me until I was quite familiar with the entire
gestalt of their behavior. Since then, Stephenson (1973) has
described similar variations of these patterns of courtship
in feral troops in Japan.

Once the behavioral units have been defined, a method of
quantifying them must be selected. Whatever the method, the
primary consideration is the reliability of the data. The
methods must be such that they can be repeated without bias.
Theoretically there are two basic methods: that of sampling
and that of recording in toto the behaviors of interest.
Almost all recording involves some sampling, of course, but a
distinction I wish to draw is between time sampling, that is,
recording only behaviors that occur at some specified period,
for example, every 30 seconds, vs. frequency counting, or
recording each incidence of behavior whenever it occurs.
Another distinction can be made between following individuals
that are selected or sampled from a group or following the
behavior of every individual in the group. Most field
studies have used sampling techniques because not all of the
animals are under observation at any one period. Here again
is another advantage of a properly set up seminatural situation:
either or both techniques can be used to collect data. Altmann
and Altmann (1970) discuss the many biases that can enter into
sampling procedures and present some statistical techniques
for estimating the extent of such biases.

In my own work with the Oregon troop of Japanese macaques, I
have tried to record in toto the aggressive behavior of every
adult in the troop for the first three hours of light, 5 days
a week, 52 weeks a year. Four patterns of aggressive behavior
have been recorded in terms of increasing severity (cf.
Alexander and Roth, 1971; Eaton, in press): 1) threat,
lunging toward another animal, gaping or earflattening, or
emitting a "woof" vocalization; 2) chase: pursuit accompanied
by threats; 3) punish: biting of brief duration which does
not injure and/or pinning to the ground, striking, leaping on,
or pulling fur or body parts; 4) assault: biting which injures
or is prolonged and accompanied by vigorous head movement while
the teeth are gripping the victim. If more than one type of
behavior occurs during a single sequence, only the most severe
is scored, e.g., if one animal chases, catches, and punishes
another, only a punish is scored. For each incident of

aggression, one of three forms of response is also recorded:
1) <u>submission</u>: moving away, grimacing, cringing, or crouching;
2) <u>stand-off</u>: submission not apparent or submissive gestures
interspersed with aggressive actions; 3) <u>ignore</u>: no aggressive
or submissive behavior in response to the attack. Scott (1958)
emphasized the importance of specifying the stimulus (attack)
and response (submission, etc.) of aggressive behavior and has
referred to the total pattern of threat-attack-submission-flee
as "agonistic behavior."

We observe the troop from an observation tower and record on
tape every agonistic interaction that involves an adult macaque.
The tape is then transcribed and the data keypunched so that
there is one interaction per computer card. The four classes
of attack described above are assigned the numbers 1 to 4 and
the three forms of submission, 1 to 3. A typical computer card
might then contain the sequence 01157408130170280401 which
indicates that on January 15, 1974, at 8:13 a.m., a female
named Infinity (No. 017) attacked another female named Twiggy
(No. 028) in a manner defined as an <u>assault</u> (04) and that
Twiggy responded with <u>submission</u> (01).

The next step is to analyze the data in such a way as to answer as accurately as possible the previously quoted questions
posed by Beach (1960). How did the behavior get to be what
it is? What are its external causes, and what internal mechanisms mediate it? We have tried to deal with environmental
determinants by summarizing into a matrix format all the
recorded aggressive interactions over a specific period of
time. Thus, all the animals of interest are listed on both
axes with the attacking animals in a column at the left and
the attacked animals in a row across the top (Table 1). This
format can then be set up for different classes of animals,
different classes of agonistic behavior, and different time
periods. For example, Table 1 is taken from a study in which
I attempted to correlate the dominance rank and mating frequency of the adult males in the troop (Eaton, in press).
Therefore only the adult males were included, the time period
was the fall and winter breeding season, all four categories
of attack from <u>threat</u> to <u>assault</u> were included, and following
Sade's (1967) example, only <u>attacks</u> that were unambiguously
followed by submission were included. Cases in which more
than one attacker was involved were also omitted. The ranks
were combined to obtain a minimum number of reversals in

TABLE 1. *Dominance Rank of Adult Male Japanese Macaques Compiled from 646 Attacks in Which Submissive Behavior was Observed*

Dominance Rank	Male Number	Field Mark	Attacked Males (frequency)																						No. of Males Attacked[b]
			△	∧	▽	B	3	E	α	ৎ	⌐	—	h	ꓒ	ꓓ	F	φ	ꓡ	⋀	7	9	V	X	
1	1723	△		8	2	0	10	3	0	1	1	0	2	0	8	0	1	1	1	0	1	1	2	13
2	1751	∧			7	5	3	2	2	4	2	3	15	5	6	0	4	2	1	3	0	3	3	1	17
3	1728	▽				9	9	1	2	1	4	0	16	10	4	1	20	3	3	5	0	1	12	3	15
4	1766	B			2		5	2	6	4	3	6	0	4	5	3	5	3	3	3	2	2	13	2	16
5	1734	3				1		3	9	1	3	12	6	5	6	2	11	0	3	2	1	4	6	0	13
6	2378	E							1	4	1	0	0	4	1	0	0	1	1	1	1	1	0	1	9
7	1725	α						1		0	0	0	0	1	1	0	3	0	0	0	1	1	6	0	8
8	3223	ৎ									1	21	0	1	1	3	3	0	0	0	0	0	1	0	4
9	1719	⌐										1	1	1	0	0	1	0	1	0	0	0	6	2	9
10	3302	—											2	1	3	3	0	2	0	0	3	1	1	0	5
11	2191	h			2						1			3	6	6	10	1	0	1	3	2	3	1	10
12	1768	ꓒ													6	6	0	2	2	3	0	9	3	1	7
13	1756	ꓓ							1		5					1	4	1	1	0	5	3	3	0	5
14	1736	F															0	0	0	0	5	0	3	1	4
15	1741	φ								1								8	5	1	1	0	6	5	5
16	1735	ꓡ																	1	0	0	0	0	0	1
17	1716	⋀							1	1	1					1				6	3	3	33	6	4
18	1733	7								1											1	1	1	1	4
19	1753	9														1							4	3	2
20	1721	V							2		3	1	2		2		2							4	2
21	1764	X										1										1	1		2
Attacked by[c]																									
No. of males			0	1	2	2	4	5	5	6	7	4	9	8	11	7	10	10	11	10	13	16	14	

[a] Entries below diagonal line indicate reversals of dominance rank.
[b] Minus those males that had more frequently attacked the male in question.
[c] Minus those males that had been more frequently attacked by the male in question.

the linear order. Ties were subsequently broken first by giving precedence to the male that had more frequently attacked the other male or if tied there, by giving precedence to the male that had been attacked by a fewer number of other males, or if a pair was still tied, by giving precedence to the male that had attacked the greatest number of other males. The reliability of this method of assessing dominance rank was demonstrated in another study in which the correlation between ranks that were determined one year apart was .98 (Eaton and Resko, unpublished observations).

The matrix format also lends itself to comparisons where inter-action effects may follow. For example, we are now investi-gating seasonal changes in aggressive behavior and are inter-ested in learning not only whether males attack other males more frequently during the breeding season but whether the proportion of males attacked vs. females attacked increases. In addition, we have divided the troop into sex and age group-ings and will analyze them month by month according to each of the categories of attack and submission to determine develop-mental patterns of sex differences in aggressive behavior.

Random sampling techniques have also been used to study the behavior of our adult males. Rasmussen (1973) divided the two-acre corral into a 6-meter square grid system and during 10-minute observation periods recorded the position and the behavior of two adult males every 15 seconds. The locations were numbered sequentially on a map of the corral so that the direction of movement and the location of the recorded be-haviors could be ascertained (Fig. 1). Since there were 20 males, there were 190 possible pairs (20! /2! 18!). Consec-utive pairs were selected from a list which maximized the number of pairs before observations were repeated on either male. With these data, it is possible to determine the average distances between all pairs of adult males, their locations in the corral, their behavior in the different locations, the relative amount of area each male uses, the rate at which males are near to or in contact with other males, females, juveniles, and infants, and the rate of certain agonistic and affiliative behaviors. Preliminary analysis indicates a very low rate of aggression between males relative to the amount of time spent in other activities. Subordinate males were observed to maintain distances by avoiding dominant males when they were moving rapidly or otherwise signaling

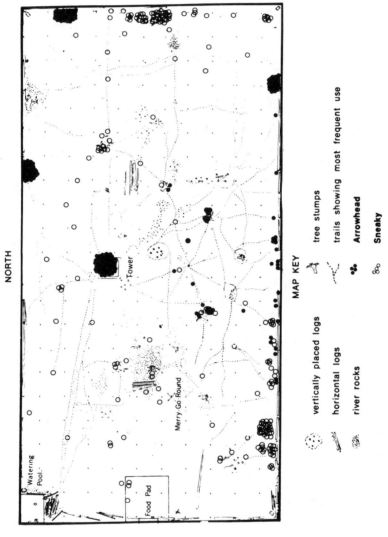

Fig. 1. This composite map was drawn from six 10-minute samples of the locations of Arrowhead, the alpha male, who prefers to sit on top of the tower and in the east end of the corral, and Sneaky, a low-ranking male, who is almost always moving about the corral. Specific locations were recorded every 15 seconds. Taken from Rasmussen (1973).

increased probabilities of aggressive behaviors. Much of the
data is of animals resting or walking quietly from one area
of the corral to another, but they are quantified objective
records of the social system functioning efficiently. Such
spacing demonstrates the social system working; agonistic
encounters and dominance interactions demonstrate its establishment or maintenance (Rasmussen, 1973).

The final step in the study of primate aggressive behavior
under natural or seminatural conditions is to introduce manip-
ulative procedures. Schneirla (1950) and Mason (1968) emphasized the close relationship between observation and experimentation in the field study of behavior through the effective
control of conditions in both stages of study. "The fundamental precautions directed toward adequacy of preliminary
observations thus provide a basis for a later introduction of
systematic changes designed to explore what may be termed the
inner nature of the phenomenon." (Schneirla, 1950, p. 1023).
Herein lies perhaps the ultimate value of studying animals in
a seminatural enclosure: the potential for controlled experimental manipulation.

Alexander and Roth (1971), who studied the relation between
crowding and aggression in the Oregon troop, emphasized the
difficulty of studying the relationship carefully in man and
other primates because of the many variables that can be
confused with space restriction. They therefore modeled their
experiment on a study by Southwick (1967) in which the space
available to a group of rhesus monkeys in a large outdoor
cage was halved. This method minimized the stress of transportation and the novelty of the new environment.

The Oregon troop had been captured intact in the wild and had
been left undisturbed in a two-acre enclosure for 2-1/2 years
before the experiment. Thus, Alexander and Roth were able to
observe the effects of crowding on a well-structured, stable
social group. They constructed a 187 m^2 "crowding pen" next
to the 8,058 m^2 corral, allowed the troop free access to the
pen for a 38-day adaptation period, and then alternated three
control periods when the monkeys had access to both pen and
corral with three experimental periods of 4 to 6 days each
when the troop was confined to the pen.

In general, the frequency of aggression increased in the
crowded conditions. However there was no breakdown in the

social structure of the troop and the dominance hierarchy was
more predictive of aggressive events in the pen than in the
corral. Moreover, these workers concluded that an increase
in severe aggression was due more to the removal from a familiar habitat than to increased density and that crowding per se
produced an increase in mild aggression. This hypothesis was
deduced from the fact that the number of severe attacks de-
clined from the first to the third crowded session and from
observations of troop behavior when the animals were initially
introduced into the two-acre corral 2-1/2 years before the
experiment. After the troop had arrived in Oregon, it was
confined to a 1,100 square foot colony pen. The move to the
corral after 17 months increased space by a factor of 73.
There was an immediate increase in severe aggression that
lasted about three weeks and left one male dead and three
others severely injured (Alexander and Roth, 1971).

We have experimentally manipulated the macaques only once since
this study was completed in 1969. In 1970, IUDs were placed
in some of the females to investigate which factors control
the breeding season (Eaton, 1972). The IUDs have since been
removed and no new manipulations are planned for the immediate
future because we want to observe troop behavior as the population density increases. A confined troop of natural origin
is such a valuable resource and the potential information on
the effects of a natural increase in population density are
of such interest that interference with the troop is to be
kept at a minimum. We are, however, planning to build a
second corral adjacent to the first which will provide not
only information on troop fission but the ultimate in seminatural situations for future research: an experimental and
a control troop.

The emphasis in this paper on the study of primate aggressive
behavior under seminatural conditions can be summarized under
the following general list of conceptual and methodological
procedures which are applicable to other behavior studies.

  1) Question. Define the questions that are to be
     investigated as determinants of behavior.

  2) Observe. Carefully and intensively observe the
     animals.

  3) Define. Objectively define the behavioral units
     that are to be recorded.

4) <u>Quantify</u>. Systematically and reliably record quantitative data.

5) <u>Analyze</u>. Formulate the data analysis so that the questions defined above can be answered.

6) <u>Experiment</u>. Attempt to answer hypotheses deduced from the analysis by controlled experimental manipulation.

Problems specific to primate studies are difficult to identify. If any one feature needs emphasis, it is that <u>anything</u> or <u>everything</u> can affect primate behavior. This is probably related to their intelligence, curiosity, and ability to adapt to almost any environmental conditions. It also makes experimental control of extraneous variables extremely difficult. Under most seminatural conditions, a repeated-measures design in which control and experimental periods are repeatedly alternated is the best that can be achieved. However, such a design demands that assumptions about the independence of the observations be met before statistical analyses can be performed with the data.

Acknowledgment

Publication No. 720 of the Oregon Regional Primate Research Center, supported in part by Grants HD-05969, RR-00163, and RR-05694 from the National Institute of Health, United States, Public Health Service. I thank Kurt Modahl for his assistance in observing the Oregon Troop of Japanese macaques.

References

Alexander, B.K., and Roth, E.M. The effects of acute crowding on aggressive behavior of Japanese monkeys. <u>Behaviour</u>, 1971, <u>39</u>, 73-90.

Altmann, S.A. A field study of the sociobiology of rhesus monkeys (<u>Macaca</u> <u>mulatta</u>). <u>Ann</u>. <u>N.Y</u>. <u>Acad</u>. <u>Sci</u>., 1962, <u>102</u>, 338-435.

Altmann, S.A.   Sociobiology of rhesus monkeys. II.
    Stochiastics of social communication. J. Theoret. Biol.,
    1965, 8, 490-522.

Altmann, S.A.   The structure of primate social communication.
    In: S.A. Altmann (ed.), Social Communication Among Primates.
    Chicago: Univ. of Chicago Press, 1967, pp. 325-362.

Altmann, S.A., and Altmann, J.   Baboon ecology: African field
    research. Bibl. Primat., 1970, 12, 1-220.

Beach, F.A.   Experimental investigations of species specific
    behavior. Amer. Psychol., 1960, 15, 1-18.

Carpenter, C.R.   Sexual behavior of free ranging rhesus
    monkeys (Macaca mulatta). I. Specimens, procedures and
    behavioral characteristics of estrus. J. Comp. Psychol.,
    1942, 33, 113-142.

Carthy, J.D., and Ebling, F.J. (eds.).   The Natural History of
    Aggression. London: Academic Press, 1964.

Chance, M.R.A.   Social structure of a colony of Macaca mulatta.
    Brit. J. Animal Behav., 1956, 4, 1-13.

Collias, N.E.   Aggressive behavior among vertebrate animals.
    Physiol. Zool., 1944, 17, 83-123.

Darling, F.F.   A Herd of Red Deer. London: Oxford Univ. Press,
    1937.

Eaton, G.G.   Male dominance and aggression in Japanese macaque
    reproduction. In, Reproductive Behavior, (W.A. Sadler
    and W. Montagna, Eds). New York: Plenum, 1974, in press.

Eaton, G.G.   Seasonal sexual behavior and intrauterine
    contraceptive devices in a confined troop of Japanese
    macaques. Horm. Behav., 1972, 3, 133-142.

Eaton , G.G. and Resko, J.A.   Plasma testosterone and male
    dominance in a Japanese macaque troop compared with
    repeated measures of testosterone in laboratory males.
    Unpublished ms. 1974.

Hall, K.R.L.   Aggression in monkey and ape societies. In: J.D. Carthy and F.J. Ebling (eds.), The Natural History of Aggression. New York: Academic Press, 1964, pp. 51-64.

Hinde, R.A.   Animal Behavior, 2nd ed. New York: McGraw-Hill, 1970.

Hinde, R.A., and Rowell, T.E.   Communication by postures and facial expressions in the rhesus monkey (Macaca mulatta). Proc. Zool. Soc. London, 1962, 138, 1-21.

Marler, P.R., and Hamilton, W.J.,III.   Mechanisms of Animal Behavior. New York: Wiley, 1966.

Mason, W.A.   Naturalistic and experimental investigations of the social behavior of monkeys and apes. In: P.C. Jay (ed.), Primates: Studies in Adaptation and Variability. New York: Holt, Rinehart and Winston, 1968, pp. 398-419.

Peters, M., and Ploog, D.   Communication among primates. Annu. Rev. Physiol., 1973, 35, 221-242.

Rasmussen, D.   Spatial relations among adult male Japanese macaques. Primate News, 1973, 11, 11-15.

Rothballer, A.B.   Aggression, defense, and neurohumors. In: C.D. Clemente and D.B. Lindsley (eds.). Aggression and Defense: Neural Mechanisms and Social Patterns (Brain Function, Vol. 5). Los Angeles: Univ. Calif. Press, 1967, pp. 135-170.

Rowell, T.E.   Agonistic noises of the rhesus monkey (Macaca mulatta). In: Evolutionary Aspects of Animal Communication. Symposia Zool. Soc. London, 1962, 8, 91-96.

Rowell, T.E., and Hinde, R.A.   Vocal communication by the rhesus monkey. Proc. Zool. Soc. Lond., 1962, 138, 279-294.

Sade, D.S.   Determinants of dominance in a group of free-ranging rhesus monkeys. In: S.A. Altmann (ed.), Social Communication Among Primates. Chicago: Univ. Chicago Press, 1967, pp. 99-114.

Schneirla, T.C.   The relationship between observation and
    experimentation in the field study of behavior. Ann.
    N.Y. Acad. Sci., 1950, 51, 1022-1044.

Scott, J.P.   Aggression. Chicago: Univ. of Chicago Press,
    1958.

Southwick, C.H.   Aggression among nonhuman primates. Addison-
    Wesley Modular Publications, Reading, Mass. Module 23,
    1972, pp. 1-23.

Southwick, C.H.   An experimental study of intragroup agonistic
    behavior in rhesus monkeys (Macaca mulatta). Behaviour,
    1967, 28, 182-209.

Stephenson, G.R.   Testing for group specific communication
    patterns in Japanese macaques. Sym. IVth Int. Congr.
    Primat., Vol. 1: Precultural Primate Behavior. Basel:
    Karger, 1973, pp. 51-75.

Washburn, S.L., and Hamburg, D.A.   Aggressive behavior in
    Old World monkeys and apes. In: P.C. Jay (ed.).,
    Primates: Studies in Adaptation and Variability. New
    York: Holt, Rinehart, and Winston, 1968, pp. 458-478.

DISCUSSION

Harvey:
Would you discuss the function of the aggressive behavior in your monkey troop. It does not seem to be determining any gene segregation.

Eaton:
One function seems to be population control. The troop is sensitive to increased numbers which leads to fission of the troop.

Adams:
The data from Washburn and Devore in the Kenya baboons indicate that over time there was a good deal of copulation by the low ranking males, but if you looked just at the height of estrus when the probability of fertilization was high then the high ranking males had a much higher proportion of copulations.

Eaton:
I looked at that, but there are two problems, one is in determining when estrus occurs without independent ovarian data; the other problem is that many studies have shown that monkeys copulate throughout the menstrual cycle. There is no evidence of an estrous period. In the laboratory we have found that at midcycle the female is apparently attractive to the male, but as far as receptivity is concerned, we find that the female is equally receptive throughout the cycle. Therefore, I counted back from birthdates to see if high ranking males were copulating at the time of conception. Unfortunately, the data were too scattered for statistical analysis; my clinical impression was that the high ranking males did not copulate more at that time; if anything there was a clustering of 5-6 year old males copulating at that time. This probably would not happen in the wild because these males would not be in the center of the troop.

Flynn:
Are there any pairings which occur, one individual being the recipient of aggressive behavior?

49

Eaton: Yes, one thing we see often is that when a high
              ranking animal chases a low ranking animal, the
              low ranking animal will look for another animal
              to chase. Some of the animals have a preferred
              low ranking animal they will immediately head
              for if they are chased.

Plotnick: Would you comment on the lack of correlation
              between dominance and testosterone which you
              found versus other studies which seem to find
              a relationship.

Eaton: The difference may be that the dominance order
              which we find is not established by fighting.
              Thus, the males at the bottom are not stressed.
              In other studies the relationship may be due to
              stress.

Perachio: Do you find any sex differences in aggression?

Eaton: There are definite sex differences and those
              differences change comparing breeding season
              with non-breeding season. The males become
              much more aggressive during the breeding season.

Perachio: Bernstein has the impression that female rhesus
              tend to be more aggressive than male rhesus on
              the average.

Eaton: I would agree in terms of frequency, although
              not in terms of intensity.

Montagu: There are some fascinating observations in the
              relationship between crowding and aggressive
              behavior. Some years ago I was speaking with
              the Commissioner of police of Hong Kong which
              is known to be one of the most crowded areas of
              the world and I learned from him that virtually
              all crime rates including violence are low. He
              attributed this to the Chinese family, and its
              socialization process. This is an example of
              excessive overcrowding with non-aggressive
              behavior.

Eaton: Probably the normal home range of our troop
                would be a minimum of 250 acres. Our animals
                are in 2 acres, so they are crowded into 0.8 of
                1% of the minimum of their home range, yet
                they are living a relatively peaceful existence.

Gorney: Do you know whether this tendency to be divided
                into dominant and subordinate groups, on other
                than a genetic basis, occurs in the wild?
                Secondly, if that does occur, can you see any
                survival implications in that? It sounds, in
                human terms, like the development of a rudiment
                of class distinction without the economic aspects
                that underlie it in our own case.

Eaton: Dominant and subordinate groups do occur in the
                wild. With respect to the second question, no
                one has studied what happens to the peripheral
                males, whether they go into other troops and if
                so, what do they do. This would have implications
                for the question. Finally, this does seem to
                be a rudiment of a caste system in that rank
                is perpetuated generation through generation.

Gorney: What would be its survival benefit?

Eaton: It could function to control access to food
                during difficult times. It is not likely to
                function as a defense against predators.

EXPERIMENTAL ANALYSIS OF AGGRESSION AND ITS NEURAL BASIS

John P. Flynn

Department of Psychiatry

Yale University

New Haven, Connecticut

At the present time there is no universally accepted definition of aggression, but one could probably get some agreement that threat and attack, even when done in the course of defense, are matters of major interest. Most would also say that exchanges between members of the same species were of particular importance. If we take this as a starting point for our inquiry into the neural basis of aggression, we are immediately confronted with the fact that what knowledge we have of the topic is not restricted to exchanges between members of the same species. There are two kinds of behavior whose neural basis is relatively clear. The classical rage syndrome seems to be defensive behavior in which threat and attack are major elements. The animal defends itself against various species, as potential sources of danger. On the other hand, quiet attack which is highly lethal, and relatively devoid of threat, is directed against members of the same and of other species.

Historically, the literature dealing with the neural basis of aggressive behavior focusses more on anger and rage than

on aggressive behavior. The focus was mainly on the single
animal and not on the exchange between animals, which would
seem to be a necessary requirement for the study of aggressive
behavior. A physiologist customarily uses the single animal
and its actions as the object of his experiments and physiol-
ogists have provided most of the relevant data. The result
has been that the kind of approach used in the study of
dominance and its establishment was not employed in research
dealing with the neural basis of aggression until 1954, when
Rosvold, Mirsky and Pribram (1954) observed the behavior of
monkeys while they were taking food from the experimenter.
Previously there were interchanges observed usually between
the experimenter or some other human being, or possibly
between a cat and a dog, or on occasion two cats, or the
response of the animal to a stick or a glove presented to
the animal, but these were incidental observations rather than
the major focus. The first systematic study of attack was
that of Karli (1956-57), who dealt with the rat's attack on
a mouse.

The phenomenon directly observed earlier was a display, that
constituted the signs expressive of anger or rage and also
was recognized as being a defensive response much as a cat
might make when confronted with a barking dog. Cannon and
Britton (1925) basing themselves on Woodworth and Sherrington
(1904), give the following description of the phenomenon:
"These quasi emotional phenomena included lashing of the tail,
arching of the trunk, thrusting and jerking of the restrained
limbs, display of the claws and clawing motions, snarling and
attempts to bite. These were also actions due to skeletal
muscles. Besides these, and more typical and more permanent,
were effects on the viscera, produced by impulses discharged
over the sympathetic nerve fibers. They included erection
of the tail hairs, sweating of the toe pads, dilation of the
pupils, micturition, a high blood pressure, a very rapid
heart beat, and abundant outpouring of adrenalin, and an
increase in blood sugar." The common and prevalent idea that
the signs expressive of rage were accompanied by affective
feelings, provided the parts of the brain necessary for
the perception of such feelings were intact, was challenged
by Masserman (1941), who wished to know if otherwise intact
animals displaying rage elicited by electrical stimulation of
the hypothalamus were in fact experiencing anger. One of his

principal tests for subjective experience was related to
learning. He held to the notion that learning implied a
conscious experience. He tried to establish a response to
a previously ineffective stimulus, like a sound or light,
paired with stimulation of the brain first in lightly
anesthetized animals to see if this could be done without
consciousness, and second, while the cats were unanesthetized.
He considered the failure in the second instance to indicate
that there was no conscious feeling involved and, therefore,
the signs expressive of rage were a motor phenomenon devoid
of feeling. The same general kind of test was later used by
Nakao (1958), who was successful and drew the opposite
conclusion. At an earlier date, Hess (1943), who saw that
cats directed their threats at him, and sometimes attacked
him, had rightly opposed Masserman's position (Hess and Akert,
1955).

The trend to the study of exchanges between animals in
relation to the neural basis of aggressive behavior began in
1954 with the work of Rosvold, Mirsky and Pribram, on shifts
in dominance following removal of the amygdala. This sort
of work is still relatively restricted even though it was
used early in behavioral studies and in studies of the effects
of hormones on dominance. Other work in which the interchanges
between animals were a focus began more or less independently.
In this same decade Karli (1956-57) initiated his studies of
the killing of mice by rats and assessed the effects of
removing frontal cortex on this behavior. Von Holst and
von St. Paul (1963), ethologists whose knowledge of naturally
occurring behavior was considerable, observed the exchanges
between chickens, which were induced by stimulation of the
brain of one of the two animals. The attacks of a chicken
upon an assistant or on a stuffed polecat were also studied.
Even though they were inactive, these last were referred to
as predators. Conceptually, one might consider the experimenter in earlier studies as having this same role. Akerman
(1966) stimulated the brains of pigeons, and using the etho-
logical analysis of Fabricius and Jansson (1963), distinguished
two forms of attack. Wasman and I (1962) found two kinds of
attack, which cats employed in attacking a rat, while the cat
was being stimulated at appropriate sites in the brain. One
was a defensive threat and attack, which was the classical
form of affective defense discovered by Hess (1928), and the

other was a more lethal form in which the cat quietly
approached a rat and bit it in the back of the neck. These
two forms have also been observed in the course of a rat's
attack on a mouse.

The model of pain-induced aggression, in which two rats
shocked through the feet fight with one another has been used
to some extent in the investigation of the neural basis of
aggression. There is quite good agreement in terms of neural
structures between those relevant to defensive threat and
attack and pain-induced aggression. With respect to this
last behavior, one would like to know what are the factors
that favor fighting as opposed to escape. The classical
response is not as dependent on noxious stimulation as in
pain-induced aggression. It is clear that all aversive
stimulation does not lead to attack, and yet it can give
rise to it. What mechanisms in the nervous system determine
the kind of response to be made to noxious stimulation?

There is also limited use of territorial fighting as a model
for the investigation of the nervous basis of aggression.
This would seem an excellent opportunity for the investigation
of learning in relation to aggressiveness, since it is the
animal's familiarity and use of the space, rather than the
space itself, that changes the animal's behavior towards an
opponent.

Various forms of agonistic behavior have been induced by
animals being in close proximity to one another. Structures
involved in fighting induced by forcing two rats to encounter
one another in their attempt to reach food have been investigated. Other similar situations (Marler, 1956) have been
used for the behavioral aspects of such encounters, and they
might profitably be extended to the study of neural mechanisms.

One way of inducing aggressive behavior in mice is to isolate
them. When an isolated mouse is placed with a mouse reared
in a group, it attacks the other animal in relatively short
order. The isolated mouse is more likely to sniff the other
animal, or to put its nose around the anogenital region, to
mount and climb upon the other than is the group-reared mouse.
The isolated mouse also startles more and freezes in position,
when sniffed, than does the other (Cairns, 1972). If tested

alone, the isolated mice are no more active than group-reared
animals, but they react more strongly to a puff of air or
to a tap with a cotton swab. The data support the idea that
the probability of attack is related to an escalation in the
vigor of exchanges between two animals ultimately ending in
vigorous fighting. The escalation of the exchange seems
comparable to one situation associated with murder. Killings
frequently start as quarrels which build up in intensity.
This model, which has at least some resemblance to a human
situation, has not been investigated in terms of neural
mechanisms.

The occurrence of attack as a result of removing or delaying
a positive reward is a matter of considerable interest
because deprivation becomes an adequate circumstance for the
elicitation of attack (Hutchinson, 1972). The possibilities
for investigating the influence of relatively subtle factors,
involving the neocortex or limbic structures, are great.

The study of the neural basis of aggressive behavior is still
in a beginning stage. The internal genesis of the state that
culminates in attack is largely unexplored. There is evidence
that internal conditions such as excitation of muscle
receptors may contribute to this (Malliani, et al. 1968).
The question of cyclicity has been joined to the question of
genesis on theoretical grounds, but the two need not be
associated.

It is my belief that the neural mechanism underlying aggressive
behavior may be suggested, and subjected to experimentation,
on the basis of close observation of the animal's actual
behavior. At the present time the kinds of behavior whose
neural underpinnings are emerging, are largely the classical
defensive threat and attack and the quiet wounding and killing.
Ethologists report that offensive threats and displays that
rarely culminate in wounding or killing occur quite frequently.
There is little exploration of the neural basis of such
behavior.

However, if one wished to separate out various aspects of
aggressive behavior, what stages or components make up the
overall behavior?

If one looks really at the end rather than the beginning of
the behavioral act, one would turn to the attack. In the
case of an offensive attack or predation, the likelihood is
that activity would terminate with biting. In predation
eating or possibly hoarding might occur soon after. The
actual terminal components for the cat at least are similar
in a fight between two cats and in predation (Leyhausen, 1973).
In the case of defensive threat and attack itself, escape
might follow, and the attack be mounted with claws rather
than with teeth.

Prior to attack, threat may have occurred. In predation,
threat is not likely to be used, since it can serve to alert
the prey. In defense, threat can enhance the size of the
defender and serve to ward off a potential attacker, as well
as mobilize the resources of the defender. In the case of
offensive threat, the threat may serve a role in communication,
and also in influencing the state of the organism, not only
to mobilize it, but also to maintain the central state of
the animal. These possible feedback mechanisms may be of
crucial importance.

The object threatened or attacked is selected. In defensive
behavior the selection may be minimal, being the object that
appears most threatening, in terms of size and in lack of
familiarity. In predation, the object attacked should be
edible. In offensive attack, if accompanied by threat, the
object of threat may well be a conspecific. How does the
nervous system operate in making these choices?

If an animal makes sensory contact particularly by means of
distance receptors, what causes it to approach the other? How
do the stimuli provided by the attack object elicit approach,
while other objects in the environment do not. In the case
of defense, the approach may not occur at all, except over short
distances. In the case of behavior induced by peripheral
electrical shock, the area within which fight occurs influences
the frequency of attack. It decreases as the area grows
larger (Ulrich and Azrin, 1962). With defensive threat and
attack elicited by electrical stimulation of the brain,
dummies were not attacked if they were more than a foot away
from the stimulated cat (Brown, et al., 1969). In the case
of quiet attack or offensive threat the distance, as in
predation, may be considerable.

Finally, is there approach in the absence of sensory cues provided by the object of attack? In the case of defense, such behavior is almost contrary to the whole notion, but it is compatible with predation, and possibly with quiet attack and offensive threat. A cat stimulated at a quiet attack site will go to a rat hidden in the arm of a maze (Roberts and Kiess, 1964). Siamese fighting fish, which mount displays followed by biting of the fins of other fish, will perform arbitrary tasks to have the opportunity to do so (Thompson, 1969). This sort of behavior in the Siamese fighting fish is clearly aggressive behavior as customarily acknowledged by ethologists. Other species frequently manifesting such behavior would be useful if the neural basis of it is to be determined. This question is a major one and can be phrased differently. Does the animal seek an opportunity to attack and is attack itself rewarding? Is the animal motivated to attack? Will the unharmed animal work for an attack object?

By addressing one's self to the behaviors observed, and the various stages indicated above, I believe that the neural mechanisms underlying aggression, defense and predation can be unraveled in a systematic way and further think that the last question, while of great importance, is inadequate to explain the other behaviors and that its solution will be greatly facilitated by the knowledge acquired in the course of answering the other questions raised. They will serve to illuminate not only the neural basis of aggression but, in general, contribute to an understanding of motivated acts.

References

Akerman, B. Behavioural effects of electrical stimulation in the forebrain of the pigeon. 1. Reproductive behaviour. Behaviour, 1966, 26, 323-338.

Brown, J.L., Hunsperger, R.W. and Rosvold, H.E. Defence, attack and flight elicited by electrical stimulation of the hypothalamus of the cat. Exp. Brain Res., 1969, 8, 113-129.

Cairns, R.B. Fighting and punishment from a developmental
    perspective. In, Nebraska Symposium on Motivation
    (J.K. Cole and D.D. Jensen, eds.). Lincoln, Nebraska:
    University of Nebraska Press, 1972, pp. 59-124.

Cannon, W.B. and Britton, S.W. Studies on the conditions of
    activity in endocrine glands: XV. Pseudaffective
    medulliadrenal secretion. American Journal of Physiology,
    1925, 72, 283-294.

Fabricius, E. and Jansson, A.M. Laboratory observations on
    the reproductive behavior of the pigeon (Columba livia)
    during the preincubatory phase of the breeding cycle.
    Animal Behaviour, 1963, 11, 534-547.

Hess, W.R. Stammanglien-reizzversuch. IV. Tagung der
    Deutschen Physiologischen Gesellschaft in Frankfurt. Ber.
    ges. Physiol., 1928, 42, 554.

Hess, W.R. and Akert, K. Experimental data on role of hypo-
    thalamus in mechanism of emotional behavior. Arch.
    Neurol. and Psychiat., 1955, 73, 127-129.

Hess, W.R. and Brugger, M. Das subkortikale Zentrum der
    affektiven Absehrreaktion. Helvetica Physiologica and
    Pharmacologica Acta, 1943, 1, 35-52.

v. Holst, E. and v. St. Paul, U. On the functional organisa-
    tion of drives. Animal Behaviour, 1963, 2, 1-20.

Hutchinson, R.R. The environmental causes of aggression. In,
    Nebraska Symposium on Motivation (J.K. Cole and D.D. Jensen,
    eds.). Lincoln, Nebraska: University of Nebraska Press,
    1972, pp. 155-181.

Karli, P. The Norway rat's killing response to the white
    mouse: An experimental analysis. Behaviour, 1956-57,
    10, 81-103.

Leyhausen, P. Verhaltensstudien an Katzen 3. Berlin und
    Hamburg: Paul Parey, 1973.

Malliani, A., Carli, G., Mancia, G. and Zanchetti, A.
    Behavioral effects of electrical stimulation of group 1
    muscle afferents in acute thalamic cats. J. Neurophysiol.,
    1968, 31, 210-220.

Marler, P. Studies of fighting in chaffinches (3) Proximity
    as a cause of aggression. British Journal of Animal
    Behavior, 1956, 4, 23-30.

Masserman, J.H. Is the hypothalamus a center of emotion?
    Psychosomatic Medicine, 1941, 3, 3-25.

Nakao, H. Emotional behavior produced by hypothalamic
    stimulation. American Journal of Physiology, 1958, 104,
    411-418.

Roberts, W.W. and Kiess, H.O. Motivational properties of
    hypothalamic aggression in cats. J. Comp. Physiol. Psychol.,
    1964, 58, 187-193.

Rosvold, H.E., Mirsky, A.F. and Pribram, K.H. Influence of
    amygdalectomy on social behavior in monkeys. J. Comp.
    Physiol. Psychol., 1954, 47, 173-178.

Thompson, T. Aggressive behavior of Siamese fighting fish--
    Analysis and synthesis of conditioned and unconditioned
    components. In, Aggressive Behaviour (S. Garattini and
    E.B. Sigg, eds.). New York: John Wiley and Sons, Inc.
    and Amsterdam: Excerpta Medica Foundation, 1969, pp. 15-31.

Ulrich, R. and Azrin, N. Reflexive fighting in response to
    adversive stimulation. Journal of Experimental Analysis
    of Behavior, 1962, 5, 511-520.

Wasman, M. and Flynn, J.P. Directed attack elicited from
    hypothalamus. Archives of Neurology, 1962, 6, 220-227.

Woodworth, R.S. and Sherrington, C.S. A pseudaffective reflex
    and its spinal path. Journal of Physiology, 1904, 31,
    234-243.

DISCUSSION

Potegal: You said that one of the criteria for assigning a behavior to the catagory of predation was the consuming of prey. As I understand the ethologist Ewer, predation involves killing and as a consequence of experience this becomes linked to eating. This connection occurs during the course of development.

Flynn: There is no question that killing behavior can go on in the absence of eating. However, predation is dismissed by some because it supposedly is based on hunger in contrast to anger or rage. For those who hold to this, eating should be a requirement for predation.

Whalen: Are there any differences in the motor patterns associated with killing followed by eating and the so-called "surplus" killing? That is, can one predict that the prey will be eaten?

Flynn: No, not to my knowledge. There is relatively little close observation available to answer that specific question.

Miczek: We have heard two contrasting views of analyzing aggression, yours and Dr. Eaton's, one describing the somatomotor patterns and one focusing on the consequences of each act. Is there a conflict here?

Flynn: I don't think there is any contradiction between the two of us. The sort of analysis I was most concerned with was one that would be suggestive of neural mechanisms. It means more to me to say that the cat's forelimbs are extended and its hind limbs flexed and its back straight than that the cat is sitting. I can deal with the former description in neurological and neuroanatomical terms better than I can with the concept of sitting.

Potegal: One way of getting from the concrete behaviors
            into the realm of motivation would be to add one
            more quantifiable parameter, the parameter of
            time. If you think about the neural mechanisms
            which govern the timing you might have a way of
            getting into something that looks like motivation.

Flynn: To appeal to motivation in the beginning seems a
            mistake because it is the same sort as the appeal
            to anger or rage. There is nothing known about
            the neurophysiology of motivation per se. I
            cannot go to a common base of knowledge about
            motivation to elucidate the rest of the behavior.

Hoebel: I would like to try to convince you that we should
            go that extra step and include motivation in our
            concepts. We look at self-stimulation and
            stimulation-escape and relate them to feeding and
            mating. It seems likely that these mechanisms
            will have some common neurophysiological elements.
            The common elements need a name, and motivation
            seems as good as any. I think that there is in
            the brain a motivation mechanism which guides the
            animal's behavior and that it stops our thinking
            to deny such a common mechanism or at least it
            helps our searching to admit that there might be
            such a common mechanism and that we can measure
            it neurophysiologically. This requires studying
            several behaviors and finding the common elements
            and then attaching such a title. It seems there
            is no harm in attaching the title before we find
            the mechanism.

Flynn: This has always been one of the arguments, that is,
            motives are supposed to simplify. I would prefer
            to see an analysis done of different kinds of
            behavior and look at the similarities in terms
            of the mechanisms, then, if we find similar
            mechanisms, we can apply the term "mechanisms of
            motivation."

Plotnick: If an electrode elicits quiet attack on a rat
            and you put that cat in with another cat, does
            the electrical stimulation then elicit the same
            pattern or does the pattern change?

Flynn: There is some slight change. If the cat stalks
                a rat, that cat will continue to stalk another
                cat. There is some interaction between the object
                and the cat that is being stimulated, that is, the
                cat that is being stimulated is responsive to the
                objects in the environment. Nonetheless, the
                basic patterns are similar.

NEUROPHYSIOLOGICAL APPROACHES TO THE STUDY OF AGGRESSION

Adrian A. Perachio and Margery Alexander

Emory University, Atlanta, Georgia 30322

The development of techniques for the neurophysiological
investigation of the unanesthetized central nervous system
of behaving organisms has provided a number of important
innovations for the study of aggression. In this presentation, I will discuss two methods: electrical stimulation
and electrophysiological recording of the activity of the
central nervous system. Of these, the former has been more
widely applied in research on aggressive behavior. Thus
far, recording methods have been used relatively infrequently. A discussion of the advantages and limitations of
each of the two approaches may offer some reasons for the
apparent difference in popularity of the two techniques and
may indicate how each set of methods may be used in future
research in the problem area of the neural mechanisms underlying social aggression.

Neurophysiological investigations of aggression most frequently have addressed the problems of either electrically
evoked agonistic interactions between different species or
attack responses directed toward inanimate objects. This
work has been reviewed extensively (Flynn et al., 1970;
Flynn, 1972; Clemente and Chase, 1973; Kaada, 1967); moreover, many significant contributions in these areas have
been made by Dr. J. P. Flynn whose presentation will be
heard during this Workshop. Therefore, the major emphasis
of this discussion will be the evaluation of problems

related to research on evoked aggression between animals of
the same species.

ELECTRICAL STIMULATION

This method has several distinct advantages for functional
analyses of discrete portions of the intact nervous system.
There is a degree of localization of effect, in that vastly
different behavioral responses can be obtained with each
millimeter of movement of the electrode. Histological
localization of the tip of each stimulating electrode is a
simple procedure. In most species, techniques have been
worked out for both acute and chronic electrode implantation
in the unanesthetized behaving preparation. The behavioral
responses are highly repeatable and the onset of aggression
can be readily controlled. Within certain limitations, this
method can be combined with a variety of physiological
techniques as well as behavioral measurements. In a social
context, other animals that interact with the stimulated
animal as targets of the aggression evoked by stimulation
can also be the subjects of physiological and behavioral
measures that are uncontaminated by the side-effects of
stimulation. Furthermore, the social setting allows the
investigator an opportunity to vary systematically group
composition and environmental factors.

There are, however, a wide variety of limitations to this
technique. First and foremost, the stimulus is a non-
physiological one. Electrical stimulation of the complex
of neurons in the brain can produce activation of cells by
orthodromic and antidromic conduction resulting in problems
in anatomical localization of the observed effect. Furthermore, axons of passage emanating from distant soma can be
activated easily by the spread of current during stimulation.
The synchronization of elements induced by each pulse of
stimulation may seriously distort the normal pattern of
functioning of the affected neural elements.

Secondly, the technique of electrical stimulation is un-
usable in some areas of the central nervous system. For
example, relatively low current stimulation of structures
in the temporal lobe, in particular nuclei of the amygdala
and areas within the hippocampus, is sufficient to produce
synchronization resulting in at least localized seizures if

not a spread of effect culminating in a manifest involvement
of the motor system in tonic-clonic seizure activity. Some
areas of the brain stem contain large myelinated axons that
pass close to, but are anatomically unconnected to cell
aggregates, particularly in the border areas of the posterior
hypothalamus. These axons have particularly low thresholds
for electrical stimulation resulting in marked muscular
contractions producing torsional movements of head, eye, neck
and shoulder. The motor responses are in some cases quite
pronounced and, in the unrestrained animal, prevent any
effective directed attack toward other members of the group.

Additional limitations arise from the use of stereotaxic
techniques for placement of stimulating electrodes. In some
species, particularly the rhesus monkey, stereotaxic atlases
are notoriously inaccurate, in part because of large individual differences in bone structures that act as reference
points for the traditional Horsley-Clark coordinate system.
Some adjunct procedures have been developed for use with
stereotaxic atlases that improve the accuracy of electrode
placement. One such procedure involves electrophysiological
monitoring during electrode implantation. When the target
area borders on a sensory structure, evoked potentials can
be produced by the appropriate stimuli; this is most easily
accomplished with visual, auditory and somasthetic stimulation.
For example, accuracy of electrode placement in the preoptic
area can be improved by detecting the ventral limits of this
region by monitoring flash evoked responses in the optic
chiasm. In addition, one can measure resistance across the
tissue-electrode interface by passing subthreshold pulses
through a Wheatstone bridge in which the electrode acts as
the unknown (Robinson, 1962). This method allows an approx-
imation of major bundles of myelinated fibers, e.g., corpus
callosum, anterior commissure, optic chiasm, etc. In contrast to myelinated areas, the cerebral ventricles represent
low impedances. Tissues composed of both cell bodies and
fibers are characterized by intermediate resistance values.
Combinations of evoked potentials and impedance measurements
can be used to greater advantages. These techniques are
most useful for detection of variations of the ventral surface
of the brain and the anterior-posterior boundaries of major
fiber pathways and sensory nuclei. In addition, variations

of electrode coordinates in parasagittal planes can be
detected by X-rays that illustrate the position of the
electrode with respect to midline structures.

The intensity of the aggressive response itself places certain limitations on the use of the stimulation technique.
When fighting does occur, the exteriorized portion of the
implanted electrode array must be secured so that the preparation is not destroyed by damage to the implant through
impact. Moreover, during episodes of intense aggression,
cables that connect the animal in a hard-wired fashion to
the stimulating apparatus can become tangled and broken.
This then requires either physical restriction of the animals
or the use of apparatus that is remotely controllable. The
latter approach has been described elsewhere (Perachio et al.,
1973). In some individual animals, in all species, the life
expectancy of the implant is shortened by the development of
granulation tissue which eventually causes sloughing of the
implant. The factors that are involved are not fully understood. Some nursing care may alleviate the problem in individual subjects; however, the problem appears to some degree
in a significant number of subjects. Non-primate mammalian
species do not seem to be particularly troubled by any tissue
reaction to the implant; however, non-human primates, perhaps
in part because of contamination of the wound margin during
social grooming or grooming by the animal itself, seem to be
most susceptible to this problem.

Finally, the behavioral response evoked by electrical stimulation of the central nervous system is most difficult to
interpret as a primary effect of stimulation. One can
postulate multiple conditions produced by stimulation that
can lead to manifest behavior of aggression: a) Centrally-
induced pain may account for biting and defensive responses
since similar behavior is readily produced by a known pain
stimulus. b) Perceptual distortions may be evoked that
produce attack or defense in response to an alteration in
the stimulus value of objects in the environment. c) Motor
effects produced by stimulation may resemble some components
of agonistic behavior. d) The evoked behavior may be a
result of the increased probability of occurrence of a set
of operant responses that the stimulated animal can perform

in the test situation. e) The stimulus may produce an
affective state that is manifested by appropriate and directed aggressive behavior that is species-specific in terms of
the response to any given stimulus object.

The technique of electrical stimulation is acceptable if it
is viewed as a preliminary attempt to assess the functional
role of particular regions of the brain. The results of
such experiments can be useful in planning research employing
techniques or physiological measures that are not complicated
by the side-effects and artifacts of electrical stimulation.

CLASSIFICATION OF EVOKED AGONISTIC RESPONSES

1. In socially isolated animals, stimulation of regions in
the hypothalamus, midbrain and amygdala produces somatic and
autonomic signs characteristic of each species similar to
its behavior during spontaneously occurring episodes of
aggression. This has been labelled affective defense. For
example, in the cat, stimulation in the appropriate areas
produces arching of the back, ear flattening, pupillary
dilatation, vocalizations and hissing with or without an
appropriate object of attack (Hess and Brugger, 1943; Wasman
and Flynn, 1962). Similarly, behavioral responses can be
obtained in both the restrained and unrestrained rhesus
monkey from stimulation of the anterior and lateral areas of
the hypothalamus that resemble components of threat and
display behavior exhibited by high ranking animals in aggressive encounters within a social group (Alexander and
Perachio, 1973). These responses, some of which can also be
observed when the animal is restrained in a primate chair,
include piloerection, pupillary dilatation, open-jaw threat,
vocalizations, limb-shaking and threat posture. Similar
responses can be seen in a social setting. In some cases,
especially with suprathreshold stimulation, the display
behavior may be escalated into a directed attack, however,
in other stimulation sites, only display components and
autonomic responses are evoked even with maximal stimulation
values. A variation of this type of response is most often
seen in a social context when the stimulated animal is
socially dominant. In monkeys, this includes threatening
and chasing without contact and does not appear to be
directed toward particular members of the group though

proximity may be an important factor in determining which
animal will be threatened first. In some cases, depending
on the dimensions of the cage and the ability of the other
members of the group to escape, contact may be made but is
not prolonged and does not include biting attack. Most often
the stimulated animal will simply make contact with his hands
and quickly disengage, directing his attention to another
animal or resuming display behavior.

2.   Stimulation in adjacent areas of the hypothalamus and in
a number of structures throughout the brain stem can evoke
flight or fear-like responses that appear to be the opposite
of affective defense and display postures. Behaviors in this
category include squealing vocalization, running and mydriasis,
salivation, piloerection. When the animal is allowed to
control stimulation, escape responses are readily conditioned.
Avoidance responses seem difficult to condition, especially
with hypothalamic stimulation (Wada et al., 1970). We have
observed in chair-restrained monkeys, that stimulation in
the posterior hypothalamus, dorsal to the mammillary bodies,
produces autonomic signs that are accompanied by an increase
in muscle tonus in the upper and lower limbs and a rigidity
of posture. When the same site is stimulated in the unrestrained subject, the animal is observed to move rapidly
around the cage, in some cases unable to avoid impact with
perches and other animals. Physical encounters with other
members of the group can result in aggression directed toward
the stimulated animal, however, no response is made by the
stimulated monkey other than escape followed by continued
rapid locomotion. With subsequent stimulations some animals
have been observed to alter their running pattern to avoid
encounter with dominant members of the group and thus,
aggression is reduced.

3.   The most intense category of behavior produced by stimulation is contact aggression. In cat, a biting attack
(with and without affective display) on an unanesthetized
rat can be produced by stimulation of appropriate areas in
the hypothalamus. In monkey, attack responses by both
dominant and subordinate animals are directed toward both
inanimate objects and other members of the group with stimulation of the anterior and lateral portions of the hypothalamus. Thus, stimulation may evoke both predatory attack

and attack by an animal toward other members of its own species resulting in intense fighting behavior that can produce serious injury.

Test Procedures

Testing conditions can alter behavioral responses produced by stimulation. Both social and environmental factors can modify the response qualitatively. Such alterations may lead to interpretative errors on the part of the investigator, and thus, both social conditions and physical environs must be considered carefully, especially in an investigation of the agonistic nature of responses obtained by stimulation techniques. Some examples have already been alluded to briefly. The following test conditions will be discussed to illustrate the problems that can be encountered in characterizing the evoked responses in unanesthetized animals, in behavioral terms: 1. Restrained 2. Unrestrained: Non-Social 3. Unrestrained: Social.

1. Restrained Conditions: The most direct and procedurally simplest means of investigating behavioral responses to brain stimulation is in a preparation that is physically restricted. The need for restraint varies with the species used. Most investigations with non-human primates have involved the use of a restraining chair or harness. Under such restraint conditions, tests with inanimate objects have been devised to measure behavioral responses during stimulation. Among the responses classified as components of agonistic behavior are grimaces, threats, avoidance or escape, biting, grasping and vocalizations.

In the restrained, socially isolated preparation, a number of interpretative problems confront the investigator when estimating the significance of the data obtained under those conditions in terms of social behavior. Restrained animals are not subject to the same social factors that regulate aggression in a group. For example, one cannot reliably predict, on the basis of the non-contact aggressive responses made by separately caged or restrained primates, the dominance relationships that will form when the animals are placed in a social group. Social status is both established and maintained by some degree of contact aggression.

Apart from social factors, behavior is modified in the restrained animal by the limitations imposed upon it with
regard to the type of responses it can produce. A stimulus
that creates a state of arousal may cause struggling and
biting in a restrained subject; however, greater freedom of
movement can enable the unrestrained animal to respond with
a wider range of behaviors in response to the same stimulus.
In addition, the constraints imposed upon the behavior of
the restrained subject may lead to qualitative misinterpretations. For example, arousal and biting evoked under restrained conditions may be replaced by flight or escape
responses to the same stimulus when the animal is freely
moving. Tests under restraint may obscure the alternatives
the animal may choose when freed from physical restrictions.
Evoked biting responses have been compared with similar
behavior induced by the pain of electrical shock to the skin.
In our experience, such comparisons have been found to be
misleading. First, we have found that individual rhesus
monkeys often bite when offered non-food items. An arousing
stimulus (e.g., sound, approach of the object, etc.) as well
as electrical stimulation of many sites that produce alerting
will result in biting. Secondly, this class of responses is
not necessarily related to agonistic behavior since a qualitatively different response may be produced by the same
stimulus parameters when the same electrode is stimulated in
the unrestrained socially interacting monkey. Finally, an
interactive effect of a qualitative nature can occur between
the animal and the investigator. Thus, the presence of a
threatening person may alter responses as compared to those
obtained by a familiar investigator. These observations
have been made in rhesus monkeys and may not be applicable
to non-primate preparations; however, they reinforce the
contention that social variables may be prepotent as determinants of evoked behaviors.

2. Unrestrained Non-Social Conditions: Physical restraint
can be minimized especially with smaller species. Small
primates can with shock avoidance conditioning or through
the use of sturdy cables, be prevented from damaging the
connections to the stimulator. All other mammalian species
seem to adapt easily to such connections and are only restrained by the length of the cable. Sufficient freedom of
movement is allowed for most species to be tested in a chamber

of limited dimensions. These methods have been used by a number of investigators, especially in tests of interspecific aggression. When it has been necessary to test attack responses within a species, the problems of avoiding damage to the connections between the stimulated animal and the apparatus have been dealt with by confining the fighting to a limited space and in some cases, by harnessing the two subjects.

In the partially restricted or unrestrained subject, tests can be made of evoked behavior involving observations of the responses in socially isolated subjects. Systematic variation of the stimulus environment has been used to investigate the preferential response to inanimate and animate objects. These manipulations have been used to distinguish feeding behavior from predatory attack in cats (Flynn, 1967) and opossums (Roberts et al., 1967). The quality of the object attacked, in terms of its sensory cues, i.e., visual, olfactory and tactual, has also been related to the nature of the evoked behavioral response. Flynn and his colleagues (Flynn, 1972) have systematically investigated the sensory modifications related to attack responses, in cats, induced by stimulation of the hypothalamus. They have described patterns of biting responses released by tactual stimulation of trigeminal fields that reflect alterations in those sensory mechanisms with hypothalamic stimulation. Similar tactual receptive field alterations were demonstrated in the forelimb of cats stimulated in areas that produce attack behavior. Visual mechanisms are also affected during responses produced by stimulation of the hypothalamus as demonstrated by alterations in attack evoked from a unilaterally blinded cat. Greater frequency of attack was obtained when the eye of the cat ipsilateral to the side stimulated was blindfolded (Bandler and Flynn, 1971).

This series of experiments is indicative of the range of experimentation that has been carried out in the investigation of non-social attack behavior. However, similar questions remain concerning the generalization from such data to the neural mechanisms related to social forms of aggression. Recalling the biting response in the chair-restrained monkey, we have found a wide range of responses when electrodes that produce such effects are re-stimulated in the socially

isolated, unrestrained subject. These include quiet, low-
affect behaviors (e.g., hand licking), pacing, running, cage-
directed biting, and affective display toward a mirror reflection. Responses toward inanimate objects can at times
be produced including destructive biting attack. In those
cases it has been found that re-stimulation in a social
context will usually produce attack directed toward another
monkey. However, there are other variables that must be
taken into account in considering the social agonistic
effects of stimulation.

3. Unrestrained Social Conditions: The definition of
aggression is critical for evaluation of the nature of evoked
behavioral responses in a social setting. In research with
groups of animals, most forms of agonistic responses can be
produced by stimulation. The use of such groups can offer
unique conditions for investigation of the interactions
between social status and evoked aggression. A characteristic
of many species is that social relationships are in part
regulated through agonistic behavior so as to form a dominance hierarchy. In such groups, aggression generally is
directed from higher to lower social ranks. The only group
member that receives no aggressive threats is the top-ranking
animal. Among social groups of rhesus monkeys, dominance
factors are important in maintaining low levels of contact
aggression.

The effects of stimulation can be viewed from two perspectives when considering social aggression as related to dominance behaviors. On the one hand, the experiential background of the stimulated animal and his social status within
the group, may act as determinants of the evoked responses
affecting the form and direction of evoked aggression.
Alternatively, stimulation of aggressive behavior in a social
group can produce both acute and long-lasting alterations in
the dominance hierarchy. Both types of interactions have
been found to be significant factors in evoked aggression in
rhesus monkeys. We have reported that evoked aggressive
behavior produced by hypothalamic stimulation in male rhesus
monkeys can be characterized in terms of the dominance status
and sex of the animal attacked. In heterosexual groups,
stimulated males attacked other males more frequently than
they did females. Most stimulation sites were associated

with attack of a male toward a subordinate target of either
sex than toward dominant animals (Alexander and Perachio,
1973). We have also found that low-ranking animals can be
stimulated to attack dominant males repeatedly, resulting in
a disruption or reversal of the dominance hierarchy in the
group. This contrasts with the findings of others (Plotnik,
Mir and Delgado, 1971) that stimulation of male rhesus
monkeys evoked attack only when the stimulated animal was
dominant and only following a brief train of stimulation.
Aggression was only associated with stimulation that was
aversive as defined by comparison of the operant response
for self-stimulation with responses for avoidance of electric
shock to the periphery. They also demonstrated that dominant
males would attack subordinates following peripheral shock.
The authors concluded that aggression, evoked by stimulation
of the hypothalamus, was a consequence of a response to a
centrally-induced aversive stimulus equivalent to pain or
intense discomfort. The contrast between those findings and
our results illustrates the need to distinguish responses to
noxious stimuli from the stimulus-bound socially interactive
effects that appear to be independent of pain-related
phenomena.

Furthermore, there is reason to distinguish intra-specific
aggression from evoked aggression directed toward other
species and inanimate objects. In cats, Flynn and his
colleagues (Flynn, 1972) have, in a series of experiments,
distinguished between affective attack and quiet biting
attack of anesthetized rats in terms of their resemblance to
pain-induced aggression. The former type of attack behavior
resembled responses to tail shock as measured by transfer
tests for conditioned escape. However, evoked affective
attack differed from responses to shock in terms of the type
of biting attack made on the rat and in the display behavior
exhibited. Distinctions were made between quiet biting
attack and eating, as responses evoked by hypothalamic
stimulation, by demonstrating that the former response could
be obtained by stimulation of sites that did not produce
eating at any stimulus parameters. The quiet biting attack
therefore appears to resemble a predatory attack without
components of hunger. It would be interesting to extend
those findings by testing evoked quiet biting attack responses
in cats in a social setting. Our data has led us to the

belief that a demonstration of socially directed attack, on
the part of a low ranking animal, offers several advantages
in characterizing the evoked aggression as distinguishable
from either pain-produced responses or non-aggressive food
gathering behaviors.

In summary, the results of experiments testing evoked behavior
in a variety of stimulus environments and social settings have
emphasized the need for caution in drawing conclusions about
social behaviors from observations of responses in restrained
and socially isolated subjects. Although biting responses to
painful stimuli may provide relevant data for displacement
types of aggression, one cannot legitimately conclude that
biting, produced by stimulation of the central nervous system,
is indicative of an affective state. That claim has not only
been disputed by demonstrations that biting in response to
pain is inhibited in a stimulated subordinate animal by the
presence of a dominant conspecific but also is countered by
evidence that evoked biting may be more validly associated
with mechanisms of mastication either as a motor reflex or as
a component of alimentation. Thus, one must view with reservation experiments that define biting behavior as a primary
manifestation of aggression. These precautions pertain to
experiments that attempt to correlate physiological events
with biting as an index of aggression (e.g., DeFrance and
Hutchinson, 1972).

Inhibition of Aggression

Efforts have been made to investigate the effects of brain
stimulation in terms of inhibition or disruption of ongoing
aggression. Conceptually, this is perhaps a more difficult
area in that a wide range of non-specific factors can reduce
aggression. Sterman and Clemente (1962) have reported that
stimulation of the preoptic area of the hypothalamus, producing electroencephalographic and behavioral effects similar to sleep, will also inhibit a biting attack by the
stimulated cat on an unanesthetized rat. Delgado (1967) has
reported that stimulation of the head of the caudate nucleus
in monkey and in bull prevents the occurrence of aggressive
behavior. We have noted that stimulation of the ventral
anterior nucleus of the thalamus produces gagging and vomiting
in rhesus monkeys.

During stimulation in this region, the monkey can easily be handled without danger of being bitten. In none of these cases does it appear to be justifiable to conclude that aggression alone has been adversely affected or specifically inhibited.

These effects, however, can be useful as an investigative means of disrupting a particular animal's social behavior. Delgado (1967) reported that low ranking monkeys learned to affect the alpha male's behavior by pressing a lever that produced stimulation in the head of the caudate nucleus. Though this experiment was not pursued in terms of determining any consequent social re-organization, such an experiment seems feasible. We have, replicating Sterman and Clemente's results, stimulated in the preoptic region of a dominant rhesus monkey to produce a lethargic, sleep-like behavior. Stimulation was delivered whenever the animal threatened or approached other members of the group. (The group was composed of the stimulated male, a receptive female and a subordinate male.) Across successive experimental sessions, the behavior of the other two animals toward the stimulated animal and toward each other changed in a systematic fashion. The subordinate male initially began to approach and then groom the stimulated male. This behavior is not exceptional for a subordinate male. Thereafter, however, he began threatening the female, who had been the second ranking member of the group, and eventually, was able to approach her and engage in copulatory behavior. Though little or no aggressive behavior was directed by the formerly subordinate male toward the stimulated animal, his dominance position and the behavior within the social group had accommodated to the social inactivity, produced by stimulation, of the alpha male. If this approach were to be combined with physiological measurements, it would provide a useful tool for investigation, in the non-stimulated animal, of physiological correlates accompanying altered social behavior.

Another approach for investigation of alterations in aggression has dealt with the interactive effects of stimulation of other sites on the evoked aggressive response produced by stimulation of the hypothalamus. This body of research has served to demonstrate that concurrent stimulation of a

number of regions in the brain can both enhance and depress
evoked attack responses. The effects were noted for both
quiet biting and affective forms of attack that are generally
associated with stimulation of the lateral and medial areas
of the hypothalamus respectively. Some areas, that with
concurrent stimulation were found to alter evoked responses,
were also found to produce attack responses themselves (e.g.,
preoptic areas and regions of the thalamus). In those
instances, concurrent stimulations were at stimulus parameters
both above and below threshold for the attack response.
Facilitation and suppression of attack have usually been
expressed in terms of alterations in attack latency. The
results of a number of these experiments can be briefly
summarized: Facilitation of attack responses has been
obtained from the medial preoptic area and the medial portion
of the lateral preoptic area (Inselman and Flynn, 1972); from
dorso-lateral areas of the posterior portion of the lateral
nucleus of the amygdala (Egger and Flynn, 1963); from ventral
hippocampus (Flynn, 1967); from the midbrain reticular formation (Sheard and Flynn, 1967) and from a number of areas
in the thalamus (MacDonnell and Flynn, 1968). Suppression
of the response, expressed in increased latency to attack,
has been reported with concurrent stimulation of the following
areas: periventricular preoptic areas and diagonal band of
Broca (Inselman and Flynn, 1972); the boundary of the magno-
cellular portion of the basal nucleus and medial portion of
the lateral nucleus of the amygdala (Egger and Flynn, 1963);
the medial prepyriform cortex (Siegel, Chabora and Troiano,
1972); dorsal hippocampus and during propagated hippocampal
after-discharge (Masman and Flynn, 1962; Flynn, 1967); areas
within the septum (Siegel and Skog, 1970); midbrain reticular
formation (Sheard and Flynn, 1967) and midline structures of
the thalamus (MacDonnell and Flynn, 1968). These findings
suggest the complexity of interactive effects that modulate
the proposed hypothalamic mechanism regulating attack behavior.

Physiological Correlates of Evoked Aggression

The evoked attack response can be useful for producing
experimentally-controlled conditions for measurement of
physiological parameters during fighting. These parameters
include both electrophysiological measurements and biochemical
assays. For example, this approach has been used to assess

cardiovascular changes in cats that were engaged in fighting behavior with a cat that was provoked to attack by stimulation of the central gray (Baccelli et al., 1968). The findings indicated that cardiovascular measures were significantly related to the type of muscular activity and the posture of the cats during fighting.

Endocrine measurements also offer a means of evaluating physiological responses during aggression. We have recently conducted experiments (in collaboration with Dr. Robert Rose, Boston University) to determine the consequences of evoked aggression in both stimulated and non-stimulated animals on hormonal activity. Assays of plasma testosterone levels were made both before and after hour-long sessions of evoked aggression that produced acute reversals of dominance status through stimulation of a subordinate male. These data were compared with similar measures made in blood samples taken before and after an equivalent amount of hypothalamic stimulation in the same animal restrained in a primate chair. In the latter test condition, a rise in testosterone was observed following an hour of intermittent stimulation. Post-session testosterone values, following stimulation in the social setting, were markedly greater than pre-stimulation values. A similar effect was observed in the unstimulated dominant male with whom the stimulated animal fought during hypothalamic stimulation. Thus, one can speculate that stimulation produced a neuroendocrine reflex via hypothalamic-hypophyseal mechanisms resulting in the release of testosterone; and that, the stress and exertion of fighting with stimulation in the social group, added to that effect to produce a greater increase in the amount of testosterone secreted into the circulating plasma. These experiments are examples of the potential of the technique of electrical stimulation for producing behavior in a controlled fashion in experiments that address the problems of correlating physiological variables with aggression.

Electrical Recordings

A number of procedural problems are shared by recording techniques and the methods for electrical stimulation of the central nervous system. The same mechanical problems exist for protecting implants during aggression. Accurate implantation for specific anatomical target areas is as much a

problem for placement of electrodes for recording as it is
for stimulating electrodes. The main advantage of electrophysiological techniques is that they are relatively passive
in terms of disrupting the physiology and behavior of the
organism; therefore, data obtained by these procedures may
be viewed as the product of normal functioning of the nervous
system with its orthodox patterns and anatomical pathways of
transmission.

Relatively few attempts have been made to assess electrophysiological correlates of aggressive behavior in the brain.
Several examples from the literature will illustrate the
types of experiments that have been conducted. It has been
reported that, in rats, during spontaneous attacks on mice,
hippocampal theta rhythm becomes greater in amplitude and
more regular in frequency (Vergnes and Karli, 1968). Similar
electrophysiological effects were observed with stimulation
of the lateral hypothalamus. Hippocampal seizure activity,
induced by electrical stimulation of the hippocampus, inter-
rupted spontaneous attack or delayed its onset. In squirrel
monkeys, desynchronization of spontaneous electrical activity
was observed in macroelectrode recordings preceding and
following episodes of biting that occurred spontaneously
during periods of restraint (DeFrance and Hutchinson, 1972).
Adams (1968) reported alterations in the firing of a small
number of single units in the central gray area of the mid-
brains of cats only during affective defense behavior.
Comparable effects were not obtained from those units with
a variety of stimuli. In contrast, units in the region of
the hypothalamus from which affective defense could be
obtained by electrical stimulation, did not respond during
that behavior.

These findings suggest that electrophysiological events may,
in a general sense, be correlated with complex behavior but
that specific relationships are difficult to define.

There are some conceptual limitations on the possible interpretations of electrophysiological recordings made from the
unstimulated central nervous system of an animal engaged in
aggressive behavior. Fundamentally, such data can be viewed
as correlational in its relation to behavior. This does not
allow conclusions of causal relationships between electrophysiological phenomena and behavior. Thus, even with

refinements beyond macroelectrode recordings of electro-
encephalograms and evoked potentials, one is faced with great
difficulty in relating single unit activity in mammalian
central nervous systems, in either extracellular or intra-
cellular recordings, to behavioral events as complex as
aggression. This in part may explain the reluctance of most
investigators to use this tool.

Conclusion

In this discussion, I have attempted to summarize briefly the
uses and methodological advantages and disadvantages of the
techniques of electrical stimulation and electrophysiological
recordings for the investigation of the neurophysiological
bases of aggression. The major conceptual problems for
interpretation of behavioral and physiological data have been
discussed. It was argued that the aggressive responses
produced by electrical stimulation of the central nervous
system must be characterized carefully in terms of the test
conditions and furthermore, should be distinguished from
comparable complex behaviors that are fundamentally unrelated
to the affective state.

Acknowledgment

This work was supported by NIH Grants RR00165 and NS-09688
and NASA Grant NGR 11-001-045.

References

Adams, D.B. The activity of single cells in the midbrain and
    hypothalamus of the cat during affective defense behavior.
    Arch. Ital. Biol., 1968, 106, 243-269.

Adams, D. and J.P. Flynn. Transfer of an escape response
    from tail shock to brain stimulated attack behavior.
    J. Exp. Anal. Behav., 1966, 8, 401-408.

Alexander, M. and A.A. Perachio. The influence of target sex
    and dominance on evoked attack in rhesus monkey. Amer.
    J. Phys. Anthrop., 1973, 38, 543-548.

Baccelli, G., G. Mancia, D.B. Adams and A. Zanchetti.
    Hemodynamic patterns during fighting behaviour in cat.
    Experientia, 1968, 24, 1221-1222.

Bandler, R.J. and J.P. Flynn. Visual patterned reflex
    present during hypothalamically elicited attack. Science,
    1971, 171, 3972.

Clemente, C.D. and M.H. Chase. Neurological substrates of
    aggressive behavior. Ann. Rev. Physiol., 1973, 35,
    329-365.

DeFrance, J.F. and R.R. Electrographic changes in the
    amygdala and hippocampus associated with biting attack.
    Physiol. and Behav., 1972, 9, 83-88.

Delgado, J.M.R. Aggression and defense under cerebral radio
    control. In: Aggression and Defense: Neural Mechanisms
    and Social Patterns. C.D. Clemente and D.B. Lindsley,
    eds. U.C.L.A. Forum Med. Sci., Univ. California Press,
    Los Angeles, 1967, 7, 171-193.

Egger, M.D. and J.P. Flynn. Effects of electrical stimulation
    of the amygdala on hypothalamically elicited attack
    behavior in cats. J. Neurophysiol., 1963, 26, 705-720.

Flynn, J. Patterning mechanisms, patterned reflexes, and
    attack behavior in cats. In: Nebraska Symposium on
    Motivation. J.R. Cole and D.D. Jensen, eds. Univ.
    Nebraska Press, Lincoln, 1972, 125-153.

Flynn, J.P. The neural basis of aggression in cats. In:
    Neurophysiology and Emotion. Biology and Behavior
    Series. David C. Glass, ed. Rockefeller Univ. Press,
    New York, 1967, 40-60.

Flynn, J.P., H. Vanegas, W. Foote and S. Edwards. Neural
    mechanisms involved in a cat's attack on a rat. In:
    The Neural Control of Behavior. R.E. Whalen, R.F.
    Thompson, M. Verzeano and N.M. Weinberger, eds.
    Academic Press, New York, 1970, 135-173.

Hess, W.R. and M. Brugger. Das subkortical Zentrum der
    affektiuen Abwehrreaktion. Acta. Helv. Physiol.
    Pharmacol., 1943, 1, 33-52.

Inselman, B.R. and J.P. Flynn. Modulatory effects of preoptic
    stimulation on hypothalamically-elicited attack in cats.
    Brain Res., 1972 42, 73-87.

Kaada, B.R. Brain mechanisms related to aggressive behavior.
    In: Aggression and Defense: Neural Mechanisms and Social
    Patterns. C.D. Clemente and D.B. Lindsley, eds. U.C.L.A.
    Forum Med. Sci. Univ. California Press, Los Angeles, 1967,
    7, 95-133.

MacDonnell, M.F. and J.P. Flynn. Attack elicited by stim-
    ulation of the thalamus and adjacent structures of cats.
    Behaviour, 1968, XXXI, 185-202.

Perachio, A.A., M. Alexander and L.D. Marr. Hormonal and
    social factors affecting evoked sexual behavior in rhesus
    monkeys. Amer. J. Phys. Anthrop., 1973, 38, 227-232.

Plotnik, R., D. Mir and J.M.R. Delgado. Aggression, noxious-
    ness and brain stimulation in unrestrained rhesus
    monkeys. In: The Physiology of Aggression and Defeat.
    B.E. Eleftheriou and J.P. Scott, eds. Plenum Press,
    New York, 1971, 143-222.

Renfrew, J.W. The intensity function and reinforcing prop-
    erties of brain stimulation that elicits attack.
    Physiol. and Behav., 1969, 4, 509-515.

Roberts, W.W., M.L. Steinberg and L.W. Means. Hypothalamic
    mechanisms for sexual, aggressive and other motivational
    behaviors in the opossum, Didelphis Virginiana. J. Comp.
    Phys. Psy., 1967, 64, 1-15.

Robinson, B.W. The impedance method of localizing intra-
    cerebral electrodes. Exp. Neurol., 1962, 6, 201-223.

Sheard, M.H. and J.P. Flynn. Facilitation of attack behavior
    by stimulation of the midbrain of cats. Brain Res.,
    1967, 4, 324-333.

Siegel, A. and D. Skog. Effects of electrical stimulation
    of the septum upon attack behavior elicited from the
    hypothalamus in the cat. Brain Res., 1970, 23, 371-
    380.

Sterman, M.B. and C.D. Clemente. Forebrain inhibitory mech-
    anisms; sleep patterns induced by basal forebrain
    stimulation in the behaving cat. Exp. Neurol., 1962,
    6, 103-107.

Vergnes, M. and P. Karli. Activite electrique de l'hippocampe
    et comportement d'agression interspecificique Rat-Souris.
    Comp. Rend. Soc. Biol., 1968, 162, 555-558.

Wada, J.A., M. Matsuda, E. Jung and A.E. Hamm. Mesencephalic-
    ally induced escape behavior and avoidance performance.
    Exp. Neurol., 1970, 29, 215-220.

Wasman, M. and J.P. Flynn. Directed attack elicited from
    hypothalamus. Arch. Neurol., 1962, 6, 220-227.

DISCUSSION

Molenauer: You have listed a number of points where stimulation has altered behavior. Do these go together in terms of some neural system underlying aggressive behavior.

Perachio: There do seem to be clusterings of points. The attack behaviors seem to be obtained from stimulation of the dorsolateral portions of the preoptic area; there are also attack responses elicited from the medial hypothalamus more posterior.

Harvey: Would you comment on Valenstein's type of analysis of evoked behaviors not being stimulus bound.

Perachio: In both the restrained and unrestrained animal we have systematic tests of each electrode trying to determine whether there are other responses that can be obtained. The response seems to be primarily characterized by its social effect, perhaps that's our bias, however. I think we have been able to focus on one type of response for some electrodes; other electrodes give us no social behavior no matter what the context.

Harvey: If given an opportunity to turn the stimulation on or off, which will the animals prefer?

Perachio: Some of our earlier experiments demonstrate that animals will self-stimulate at sites that produce attack behavior, but we have not pursued this.

Harvey: When animals are engaged in fighting does there appear to be a decrease in sensitivity to painful stimuli?

Perachio: The areas in the midbrain which produce analgesia
                   we have not found to cause stimulus bound attack.
                   However, these animals will fight even when
                   injured so there may be some sort of excitement
                   analgesia.

BEHAVIORAL GENETIC ANALYSES OF AGGRESSION

Gerald E. McClearn

Institute for Behavioral Genetics

University of Colorado

The emphasis should be on the plural in the title, because
there are as many different behavioral genetic approaches to
aggression as there are different fields of genetics. One
investigator might, for example, be interested in simply
establishing the fact of a genetic contribution to variability
in some aggressive behavior; others may be interested in
testing the possibility that a single locus is involved;
others may be exploring a quantitative genetic model; others
may be approaching the problem from a developmental perspective,
examining evidence that genes influence the manifestation of
the trait as the organism changes in age; still others may
be investigating mechanisms, exploring the endocrine, neurological, physiological, biochemical or pharmacological events
through which the genes manifest their influence; and still
others may be looking at the issue of aggression through the
perspective of a population geneticist or an evolutionary
geneticist.

The purpose of this paper is to illustrate some of these
approaches and some of the data. This will by no means be a
complete and exhaustive summary of the literature in the
field; only representative samples of the literature will be
mentioned. The paper will, hopefully, provide a notion of

the ways in which gentics can be employed as a variable, like
other variables, to be controlled or manipulated, to contribute to the elucidation of the particular subject matter
area of aggression. The discussion will be restricted
principally to the mouse, not just because it is the animal
I know best (although that is probably reason enough), but
also because most of the work has indeed been done with the
mouse.

Inbred Strains

Of the genetic approaches that can be used with animals, one
of the standard approaches has been the use of inbred strains.
Inbreeding is defined generally as the mating together of
individuals more closely related than would occur by random
assignment of mates. There are various degrees of inbreeding.
The type employed in generating inbred mouse strains is brother-
sister mating. The consequence of inbreeding of any degree,
be it remote or very close, is an increase in genetic uniformity
of the progeny of that mating. If inbreeding is continued in
a particular strain in sequential generations, genetic uniformity increases within that strain, and the animals approach
asymptotically a situation in which every mouse is like
every other mouse genetically. After about 20 generations of
inbreeding, all the mice within a strain will have become
homozygous at nearly all loci. That is to say, for almost
all genes they are alike in the state of that gene. Another
way of saying it is that inbreeding decreases the amount of
genetic variability within a strain. Zero variability is
approached, but never quite attained, within the strain. For
most purposes, however, this qualification is almost a quibble.
In terms of the utilization of inbred strains as a tool, we
can regard it as approximately the case that when we are
dealing with members of an inbred strain we are dealing with
animals that are genetically identical to each other. Furthermore, we can generate any number of such animals.

The oldest inbred strain is the DBA, which had its origin in
1909. In terms of human generations, this is roughly comparable
to the time of the building of Stonehenge. Many other strains
(the C57BL, C3H, RIII, BALB/c, and so on) were established
subsequently.

The use of these strains implies a logic more or less as follows. We know that as a consequence of inbreeding we will approach a condition of genetic uniformity within each strain. Each mouse possesses many thousands of genes. If we just consider it a random matter whether a particular gene gets fixed in one configuration or another, and considering only the possibility of two options for each gene (and there may be many more), then we can use simple binomial considerations to conclude that the probability of any two of the strains of separate origin having the same crystallized genotype is very small, indeed. Therefore, we can be quite confident that any two inbred strains differ genetically. We don't know how many genes differ, nor do we know the specific nature of the genetic differences, but we do know that they differ gentically. And we know that the animals within each strain are genetically identical, or approximately so. Therefore, if we rear and test these animals under laboratory environmental conditions that are as near identical as we can make them, and we find a difference between the strains, then we may conclude with considerable faith that the mean difference is due to genetic differences between the groups.

In general, the use of inbred strains in behavioral genetic research provides a stability of outcome that is sometimes not found when non-inbred strains are used. For example, C57BL mice are more active than are A mice, and this can be demonstrated in a variety of different apparatuses and in a variety of different laboratories, not only in this country but around the world. The same thing is true of alcohol preference. C57 mice like alcohol moderately well to excellently well, and DBA's will avoid it at all costs. This can be demonstrated in Berkeley and in Boulder and in Austin and in Edinburgh and in Helsinki and in various other places.

Inbred Strains in the Study of Aggression

Two nearly concurrent studies in the 1940's were the pioneer efforts in studying aggression of inbred strains of mice (Ginsburg and Allee, 1942; Scott, 1942).

Ginsburg and Allee (1942) found that C57BL's were more aggressive than BALB's in short paired encounters. They also showed that defeat and success experiences could alter an individual

animal's aggressiveness. This is an important point,
affirming that a genetic influence does not by any means
deny the possibility of an environmental influence and vice
versa. We are speaking, then, in terms of systems in which
both hereditary and environmental components exist and
coact in various ways. Thus, although it is possible to
alter the aggressiveness of C57BL's downward and it is
possible to alter the aggressiveness of BALB's upward by
various kinds of treatments, this is in no way inconsistent
with observations of "resting level" differences between the
strains.

Scott (1942), on the other hand, found that C57BL/10's (a
substrain of the C57BL's) were "pacifists." More recently,
Tellegen, Horn and Legrand (1969) found C57BL/6J's to be so
pacific that he uses them as standard "victims" in experiments
on the reinforcement value of fighting to aggressive animals.
Thus, inconsistencies were apparent from the beginning of
research in this area. To a considerable extent these have
been clarified by work done by Klein, Howard and DeFries
(1970). In this experiment, BALB mice and C57BL mice fought
in a more or less standard paired-encounter strange-cage
situation under high and low illumination conditions. In
Experiment 1, a red light was used for the low-illumination
condition. The C57BL's won 27 out of 30 fights when illumination was high, and the BALB's won 14 out of 24 fights when
illumination was low. In Experiment 2, in which illumination
was controlled simply by reducing the intensity of white
light, results were similar: 22 C57BL wins out of 25 in the
case of high illumination, and 13 BALB wins out of 19 under
low illumination. Not only is this outcome interesting from
the pragmatic point of test situation design, but it also
illustrates well the very significant phenomenon of genotype-
environment interaction. The issue of whether aggression
will be stronger under high or low illumination cannot be
settled without knowing the strain of the animals, and the
question of whether one strain is more aggressive than another
cannot be answered without specification of the illumination
conditions. A number of conditions other than illumination
that interact in this manner with genotype have been identified.
Fredericson and Birnbaum (1954), for example, found C57's to
be more aggressive than BALB's in food competition situations;
however, if allowed to live together for a period of time, the
BALB's tended to kill the C57's.

Southwick (1968) was interested in possible maternal influence
on aggressive behavior. Two strains were employed that had
previously been shown (Southwick and Clark, 1968) to differ
greatly in a composite CAF (chase, attack, fight) aggression
index. Male mice of the A strain (low aggression group) were
reared by mothers from the CFW (high aggression) strain,
and vice versa. Cross-fostering per se may have had an
influence, so an in-fostered control was provided in each
strain. Mice were taken from their own mothers and reared by
another mother of the same strain. Table 1 shows the
substantial increment, relative to untreated and to in-
fostered controls, in the aggression of these A animals in
the direction of the behavior typical of males of the foster
mother's strain. In-fostering had no effect. By contrast,
however, the CFW young who were reared by A mothers scored no
differently from the CFW offspring reared by either their own
or foster CFW mothers. Here, then, is another example of a
genotype-environment interaction

Table 1

Cross-Fostering and Aggressive Behavior in Two Mouse Strains

	Strain	
Group	A/J	CFW
Cross-fostered	26.6	65.1
In-fostered control	17.5	68.0
Untreated control	14.2	67.6

Source: From Southwick, Communications in Behavioral Biology,
         1968, 1(A), 129-132.

Yet another example is provided by results of a study done by
Vale, Vale and Harlye (1971), who tested the hypothesis that
stress of crowding influences aggression and certain physiological correlates. Chase, attack and fight were measured in
populations of one, two, four and eight animals of the DBA,
A, C3H, C57 and BALB strains. A striking interaction of strain
and population density was found in the attack variable. In
the case of the BALB's, there was a dramatic increase in
attacks as density increased, whereas no such trend was
observed in the other tested strains. Genotype-environment
interaction was also discovered in the relation between adrenal
gland weight and crowding. This study illustrates very well,
I believe, that the investigator who is concerned with some

dimension such as population density is well advised to
consider the nature of the animals that he is testing,
because the answer that he gets could be quite different
depending upon the genotype of the animals involved.

An interesting variant in the use of inbred material for
research purposes was employed by St. John and Corning (1973),
who were interested in female aggression. Ordinarily, female
mice are non-aggressive, and it requires special circumstances
to elicit aggression from them. A male and female of the
same strain were mated. On the 5th and 6th days after a
litter was born, one parent was removed from the cage and a
strange male was introduced. The intruder was restrained
by the tail and dangled inside the cage, providing a relatively
helpless and, to some extent, standard target. Four inbred
strains (plus a heterogeneous strain) were used. Of the males,
63% of the DBA strain, 53% of the BALB's, 13% of the C3H's and
0% of the C57BL's attacked the intruder. The principal
question was whether a female would attack under these circumstances, and, if so, whether the strain rank ordering would
be the same as in the case of the males. Of the females,
54% of the DBA's, 44% of the BALB's, and 0% of the C3H's and
C57BL's attacked the intruder. These results suggest that
the genes influencing female aggression are essentially the
same ones that influence male aggression in the mouse.

Most of the research described to this point has provided
evidence that genes may influence aggressive behavior. A
complementary approach is to examine the ways in which aggressive behavior influences the transmission of genes to the
next generation. DeFries and I (DeFries and McClearn, 1970)
investigated this matter with a live-in social situation.
Three males and three females, all strangers to each other,
are placed in a "triad" consisting of three standard cages,
interconnected by a Y-shaped plastic tunnel. Intense social
interaction occurs when the animals are thus introduced, and
both sexual and aggressive behavior begins quite quickly.
After several hours to several days, a particular social
outcome typically occurs. One male becomes dominant, and the
other two males become completely submissive. These mice
remain most of the time in one particular cage, and they only
leave that cage on pain of immediate punishment by the
dominant animal. The dominant male, is of course, free to come

and go, but often will spend much of his time in one particular cage. The females usually cluster in the third cage for sleeping, but are free to roam into any cage, including that of the subordinate males.

The prinipal question of this research was whether there was a selective advantage conferred upon the dominant male. It is entirely possible, both because dominance sometimes is not established for several days and also because the females are free to come and go as they please, that the dominant animal in these triads really does not fertilize females more often than do the other males. The participant mice were selected on the basis of coat color so that paternity could be established without ambiguity. In the first experiment, the females were BALB's and the males were inbreds of various kinds--BALB's, C57's, DBA's and A's were used in various combinations. In general, we found that BALB's and A's were more likely to be the dominant animals, C57's next, and DBA's the least likely, but these strain differences were not the main concern. Sixty-one litters were born. In several experiments, the percentage of offspring sired by the dominant male ranged from 91 to 95. This represents a stupendous Darwinian fitness, and clearly shows the extent to which aggressive behavior will be naturally selected in situations of this kind.

Selective Breeding

In selective breeding, one begins not with genetically uniform animals but with a gentically heterogeneous stock. A sample of individuals from this stock is measured on the trait of interest, and only individuals with extreme measures are permitted to mate to produce the next generation. High scoring males are mated with high scoring females, and low scoring males are mated with low-scoring females. The progeny of these two groups are then measured on the same trait--the highest scoring offspring from the high parents are mated, and the lowest scoring offspring from the low parents are mated. To the extent that the individuals' scores are influenced by their genotype, and are not exclusively due to environmental effects, a gradual separation of the means of the high and low lines will occur. If selection is continued for a sufficient number of generations, and if the genetic

contribution to variability in the trait is sufficiently
large, then the two lines may separate to the point that
there is scarcely any overlap between the distributions of
their scores.

Selective breeding has been successful for a number of
behavioral traits, including aggression. Lagerspetz (1964)
used a modification of the Hall-Klein scale (1942) to
quantify the aggressiveness of males in a paired encounter
situation. On that scale, a score of zero represented no
interest of the animals in each other, and increasing scores
represented more and more blocking, crowding, shoving and
wrestling, up to a score of six which denotes fierce
wrestling and the drawing of blood. The males who scored
highest were mated to females to make the high-aggressive
line, and the males who scored lowest were the fathers of
the next down selected generation. A problem in this situation
is immediately apparent: Females don't fight under these
circumstances, so there is no way of measuring their phenotype.
The problem is similar to that of selecting a bull for
butterfat content of milk, or a rooster for egg-laying
capacity. In this situation, the aggression scores of the
females' brothers were used to provide an estimate of female
aggressiveness. Selection proceeds more slowly in this way,
of course. Even so, the progress of selection was very
substantial--beginning with an average score of 3.4 in the
heterogeneous population, the mean of the high line rises
until, after 7 generations, it nearly reached the maximum
score possible. The non-aggressive mean drops rapidly in
the first generation, then levels off at a value of about 2.5.

Once such selected animals are available, they can be used as
tools in studying the mechanisms through which these differences
are made manifest. Table 2, for example, provides a comparison
of Lagerspetz's Turku aggressive (TA) and Turku non-aggressive
(TNA) mice on a number of neurochemical and endocrinological
measures (Lagerspetz, Tirri and Lagerspetz, 1968). TA's have
less serotonin in forebrain than do TNA's; serotonin in the
brain stem is equal, as is noradrenaline in forebrain; with
respect to noradrenaline in the brain stem, TA's have more
than do TNA's; etc. This table illustrates the potential of
selectively bred groups of animals for examining hypotheses
about the mechanisms through which genetic differences are

Table 2

Characteristics of Turku Aggressive and Non-Aggressive Mice

	TA	TNA
Serotonin in forebrain	<	
Serotonin in brain stem	=	
Noradrenaline in forebrain	=	
Noradrenaline in brain stem	>	
Testis weight	>	
Seminal vesicle weight	=	
Number and size of interstitial cells	=	
Adrenal weight	=	
Adrenalin content	>	
Amphetamine toxicity	=	
Open-field reactivity	<	
Open-field activity	>	
Wheel activity	>	
Maze learning	>	
Sexual behavior	=	
Incentive value of opponent	>	

Source: From Lagerspetz et al., Scandinavian Journal of
     Psychology, 1968, 9, 157-160.

expressed. However, there is a pitfall for the unwary. If
there are only two groups, one high and one low in aggression,
and it is discovered that, say, those high in aggression are
also higher in adrenal weight, this constitutes very weak
information. Given the high and low ranking for the one trait,
one of three outcomes must occur with respect to any other
trait. Even if no causal link exists between the two traits,
the high selected group must be either higher than, lower than
or not different from the low group in the second trait. If
a difference is found, an additional step is needed in order
to demonstrate that the association is not a fortuitous one.
That step is to observe the correlation between traits in a
genetically segregating population. Such a population can be
obtained by mating first-generation progeny (F1's) together
to get an F2. The second generation will be genetically
segregating for the genes that determine trait A and also for
the genes, if any, that are influencing trait B. If a correlation exists at this level, then the evidence for a causal

link is rather firm. (See McClearn and DeFries, 1973, p. 122, for a more detailed discussion of this point.)

I would like to close with two comments. First, my judgement is that research on behavioral genetics of aggression is now about to the point where it is ready to begin growing rapidly. Many of the problems--the conceptual problems, and the mundane problems of measurement and apparatus standardization--have been recognized and, to an extent, solved. Enough information about strain and line differences exists so that cumulative future growth can be very fast.

The second comment is that behavior genetic analysis is not an alternative to neurological analysis, or endocrinological analysis, or biochemical analysis, or behavioral analysis of aggression. It is possible to use genes as a variable to be manipulated or controlled in the conduct of these other approaches. Genes can be a most powerful tool, even for those not interested in genetics per se, to be used in illuminating their own areas of interest in the causes of aggression.

References

DeFries, J.C. and McClearn, G.E. Social dominance and Darwinian fitness in the laboratory mouse. American Naturalist, 1970, 104, 408-411.

Fredericson, E. and Birnbaum, E.A. Competitive fighting between mice with different hereditary backgrounds. Journal of Genetic Psychology, 1954, 85, 271-280.

Ginsburg, B. and Allee, W.C. Some effects of conditioning on social dominance and subordination in inbred strains of mice. Physiological Zoology, 1942, 15, 485-506.

Hall, C.S. and Klein, L.L. Individual differences in aggressiveness in rats. Journal of Comparative Psychology, 1942, 33, 371-383.

Klein, T.W., Howard, J. and DeFries, J.C. Agonistic behavior in mice: Strain differences as a function of test illumination. Psychonomic Science, 1970, 19, 177-178.

Lagerspetz, K. Studies on the Aggressive Behaviour of Mice. Helsinki: Suomalainen Tiedeakatemia, 1964.

Lagerspetz, K.Y.H., Tirri, R. and Lagerspetz, X.M.J. Neurochemical and endocrinological studies of mice selectively bred for aggressiveness. Scandinavian Journal of Psychology, 1968, 9, 157-160.

McClearn, G.E. and DeFries, J.C. An Introduction to Behavioral Genetics. San Francisco: Freeman, 1973.

St. John, R.D. and Corning, P.A. Maternal aggression in mice. Behavioral Biology, 1973, 9, 635-639.

Scott, J.P. Genetic differences in the social behavior in inbred strains of mice. Journal of Heredity, 1942, 33, 11-15.

Southwick, C.H. Effect of maternal environment on aggressive behavior of inbred mice. Communications in Behavioral Biology, 1968, 1(A), 129-132.

Southwick, C.H. and Clark, L.H. Interstrain differences in aggressive behavior and exploratory activity of inbred mice. Communications in Behavioral Biology, 1968, 1(A), 49-59.

Tellegen, A., Horn, J.M. and Legrand, R.G. Opportunity for aggression as a reinforcer in mice. Psychonomic Science, 1969, 14, 104-105.

Vale, J.R., Vale, C.A. and Harley, J.P. Interaction of genotype and population number with regard to aggressive behavior, social grooming, and adrenal and gonadal weight in male mice. Communications in Behavioral Biology, 1971, 6(A), 209-221.

DISCUSSION

van Buskirk: What is the state of information on the XYY
               syndrome and aggression?

McClearn: I think it is not proven. The data are not
               sufficiently numerous. We need better data on
               incidence in newborns and incidence among the
               "normal" population. There are some tricky
               demographic problems in this type of work.

Kessler: I would like to reinforce that statement. There
               are statements in the literature that XYY
               individuals have a twenty fold greater risk
               for becoming a criminal than an XY individual.
               The question is twenty fold in relation to what?
               If you compile all the individuals that Jacobs
               detected in institutions, and given the
               newborn rate, over 99.8% of XYY individuals are
               not in institutions. Thus, the risk for a
               XYY infant to become a criminal is rather small.

Adams: If you have several sets of coisogenic strains
               and they differ significantly in aggression or
               some other behavior, theoretically, it should
               be possible to identify the enzyme and to trace
               in the brain the action of the enzyme which is
               causing the difference. That should correspond
               to brain pathways and brain mechanisms with a
               fineness of action that is beyond any tool we
               have today.

McClearn: I agree. I think the program you outline is an
               ideal way of approaching the problem. Also you
               can selectively breed much more precisely than
               we have done in the past. If you were interested
               in the possibility that aggressive animals were
               always "X" or that "X" was strongly correlated
               with aggression you could apply an extremely
               powerful test that would be convincing in the
               negative outcome and that is to breed selectively
               for one trait while breeding in the opposite
               direction for the other. If this works then
               you know you have no necessary correlation
               between traits "A" and "B."

98

NEUROANATOMICAL TECHNIQUES FOR NEUROBEHAVIORAL RESEARCH

Gary Lynch and Herbert Killackey

University of California

Irvine, California 92664

The coupling of modern neuroanatomical techniques with more
behaviorally oriented approaches to problems of behavior and
the brain has been extremely rare. This is unfortunate, in
light of the arguments which have surrounded the interpretations
of the anatomical substrate which underlies effects noted in
various lesion and stimulation experiments (for example, the
hypothalamus and regulation of feeding behavior). In this
chapter we will discuss some of the newer anatomical techniques
and attempt to demonstrate their relevance to neurobehavioral
research.

The past ten years have witnessed a proliferation in the number
of techniques the neuroanatomist can bring to bear on the study
of the mammalian central nervous system. While it is yet too
early to tell, some of these techniques will undoubtedly prove
as fruitful as such earlier milestones in the history of neuroanatomy as: the introduction of formalin fixation by Blum in
1893 which resulted in greatly improved cellular preser-
vation; the discovery of silver impregnation by Golgi in 1875
which resulted in a vast body of data on the morphology of
single neurons and their individual processes; the introduction

by Nissl in 1894 of the cell body stain which bears his name
and made possible the study of neuronal cytoarchitectonics and
the tracing of connections on the basis of the retrograde
cellular reaction and the transneuronal cellular reaction to
injury (see Clarke and O'Malley, 1968 for a historical
overview).

The present discussion will focus on five of the new neuroanatomical techniques: namely, the Fink-Heimer technique for
staining degenerating axoplasm, the use of histochemistry for
following neural systems containing acetylcholinesterase,
iodonitrotetrazolium histochemistry for staining anterograde
degeneration, the tracing of neuronal connections based on the
uptake and transport of radioactive labelled amino acids and
the use of horseradish peroxidase for the tracing of neuronal
connections and the impregnation of neurons and their processes.
Each of these methods has its own distinct advantages and
disadvantages which will be discussed in detail below. In
describing these techniques we will stress those which are
straight forward and can be used either alone or in combination
with other anatomical, physiological and behavioral techniques
for studying the central nervous system.

The Fink-Heimer Technique

The Fink-Heimer technique for the impregnation of degenerating
axoplasm was introduced in 1967 (Fink and Heimer, 1967). It has
become the standard method for tracing axonal connections. The
technique is the last in a series of modifications of reduced
silver techniques for staining axons which were first introduced
by Cajal and Bielshowsky at the turn of the present century.
Before the introduction of the Fink-Heimer technique the method
of choice for staining degenerating axoplasm was the "suppressive"
Nauta technique (Nauta and Ryan, 1952; Nauta and Gygax, 1954).
This method with its selective impregnation of degenerating fibers
and suppression of normal fibers provided neuroanatomists with
a powerful tool for tracing central neural connections and
resulted in a wealth of new anatomical data. However, in a
number of neural systems this method was found to be limited in
its capability to demonstrate the full extent of a synaptic
terminal field. The Fink-Heimer modification of the Nauta-Gygax
method fills this gap and is believed to fully impregnate
degenerating terminal fields as well as degenerating axons along
their entire course (see Heimer 1970a, 1970b for a complete
discussion).

Since its introduction the Fink-Heimer method has been used to trace neuronal connections in a vast number of neural systems. However, most investigators have confined their interpretation of their results to simple declarative statements (i.e., Nucleus A projects to Area B) and have not fully exploited the advantages of this technique. The technique can be used not only to provide data about neuronal connectivity but also to provide insights into the physiological mechanisms which different neuronanatomical systems serve. For example, in the oppossum the Fink-Heimer technique was used to provide evidence of three separate thalamic inputs to a single region of sensory motor cortex (Killackey and Ebner 1973). Each of these inputs arose from a unique thalamic source and terminated in a unique fashion in the cerebral cortex. The first originated in the ventral posterior nucleus, was composed of large caliber fibers and terminated densely in a restricted fashion in layer IV of neocortex. The second arose from the ventral anterior lateral complex, was composed of large caliber fibers and terminated in a restricted fashion in layers IV, III, and I. The third arose from the central intralaminar nucleus, was composed of very small caliber fibers and terminated in a diffuse fashion in all cortical layers as well as in the basal telencephalic nuclei. Such analyses have also been carried out on Hedgehog somatic sensory and motor cortex (Killackey, 1972, Killackey and Ebner 1972) and are underway in the rat somatic sensory and motor systems (Killackey, 1973). In each of these systems Fink-Heimer impregnation provides a unique picture of the type and distribution of terminal degeneration suggesting that each system terminates on different types or combinations of types of cortical neurons and that each system underlies very different physiological mechanisms. Figure 1 presents photomicrographs of the two dramatically differing thalmocortical systems seen in the somatic sensory system of the rat.

One advantage of the Fink-Heimer technique is that its use can be coupled with the use of physiological techniques for studying the nervous system. Hand and Morrison (1972) have made electrophysiological records from the cat ventral posterior nucleus prior to making a small lesion for the later tracing of anterograde degeneration with the Fink-Heimer technique and then correlated the location of the receptive fields with the resultant anatomical projections. Strick (1970) has performed similar experiments in which the ventral lateral nucleus

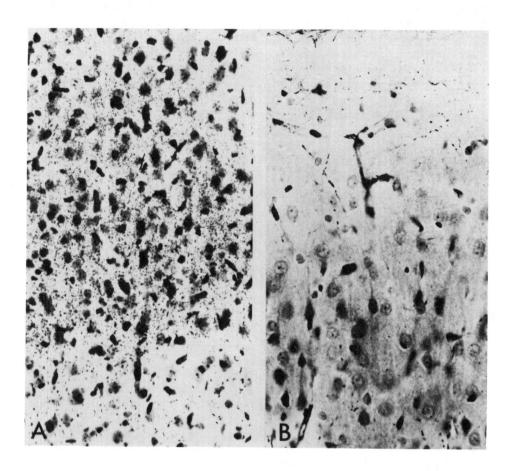

Fig. 1.   A. Photomicrograph illustrating dense restricted
terminal degeneration in layers III and IV following a discrete
lesion in the ventral posterior nucleus (VP). A receptive field
restricted to several vibrissae was recorded from the electrode
tip prior to making a lesion.

B. Photomicrograph illustrating diffuse degeneration in layer I
following a discrete lesion to cells just dorsal to VP. In this
case cells responded to pinching of the entire body surface prior
to making a lesion.

of the cat was stimulated and peripheral movements noted and
later correlated with terminal degeneration in motor cortex.
At present, similar experiments are being conducted on the rat
in an attempt to correlate receptive field properties
(restricted vs. diffuse) with the type of thalamocortical
projections seen in the somatic sensory system. At the
behavioral level, Siegel, Bandler, and Flynn (1972) have used
the Fink-Heimer method in conjunction with stimulation of
thalamic sites which elicit rage in the cat in an attempt to
outline the neuronal circuits which underlie this behavior.

Over the past several years the Fink-Heimer technique has been
employed extensively as part of an experimental paradigm to
test for neuronal plasticity in response to injury in mammalian
species. The technique has been used to demonstrate axonal
"sprouting" following the removal of neuronal inputs to a given
structure in the adult rat, (Lynch, Stanfield and Cotman, 1973)
and to demonstrate axonal "sprouting" or "directed regrowth"
following injury to the developing nervous system (cat lateral
geniculate, Kalil, 1972; rat superior colliculus, Lund and Lund,
1973; hamster nucleus lateralis posterior, Schneider, 1970; rat
hippocampus, Lynch, Mosko, Parks and Cotman, 1973). In all such
experiments an initial lesion is administered to remove a given
input, a period of time is allowed to pass for the resultant
degeneration products to disappear and a second lesion is
administered in order to study neuronal connections with the
Fink-Heimer technique. In such experiments extreme caution
must be taken to ensure that all of the original degeneration
products from the first lesion have been removed. It is
imperative that the investigator first stain a control series
of animals with the Fink-Heimer technique at varying periods of
time after the initial lesion in order to determine the time
course of the removal of the initial degenerative debris.

While the chemistry underlying the specific argyophilia of the
Fink-Heimer technique is poorly understood, the mechanics of
the stain are straight-forward and the technique can be employed
by the most basically equipped laboratory. An outline of the
technique as used in this laboratory is presented in the appendix.
The difficulty with the technique, if any, lies not with its
use, but with the interpretation of the results. Several points
which require special caution should be noted. First, the
optimal survival time varies from system to system. Consequently, a series of animals with varying survival times

following the lesion should be employed in order to determine
the optimal survival times. Second, the optimal impregnation
for a given system may vary from animal to animal. While many
steps in the stain can be changed or even omitted the use of
a trial series in which the ratios of ammonium hydroxide and
sodium hydroxide in the ammonical silver step and the amount
of citric acid in the reducer step are varied (Benevento and
Ebner, 1971) is suggested in order to determine the optimal
impregnation for a given case. Third, the investigator should
be aware of several artifacts which can be interpreted as
axonal degeneration. The most common of these are: a fine
dust-like silver deposit associated with retrograde degeneration
(Guillery, 1970), staining of the myelin sheath (this can
usually be detected by observation with a high power microscope
lens as a silver free track can be seen to run down the center
of the degenerating element) the staining of vascular elements
and the normal argyophilia of certain brain regions. Fourth,
and a more serious problem, is the inability of the method to
distinguish between nerve cell bodies and axons of passage.
Following a lesion all axons will degenerate whether they
originated at the site of the lesion or were simply passing
through this region. This can lead to serious misinterpretations
and results with the technique should always be cross checked
with other techniques. Similar precautions apply when lesions
are to be made within the central nervous system. The electrode
approach should be chosen carefully and varied in order to
ensure that degeneration which is interpreted as due to the
lesion is not in fact the result of the electrode track damaging
fibers on its course through the lesion site. Fifth, negative results (i.e., failure to find degenerating terminals) should be
interpreted with caution since there is some evidence that some
degenerating systems are not detected by the technique (e.g.,
the ascending catecholamine projections, see also Mosko, Lynch,
and Cotman, 1973). Finally, silver deposits in isolation should
never be interpreted as degeneration. The requirement which
Monakow first specified for the Marchi technique applies
equally well to other methods of determining neuronal connections.
That is, there should be a continuity of degenerative debris
between the site of the lesion and the area of suspected
terminal degeneration.

The use of Iodonitrotetrazolium (INT) histochemistry for
staining anterograde degeneration

A second approach to staining anterograde degeneration products
has recently been described (Steward, Lynch and Cotman, 1973).
This involves treating unfixed, frozen sections with the commonly
used tetrazolium salt technique for demonstrating oxidative
enzymes (Melgren and Blackstad, 1967). When this is done on
experimental material degenerating axons and terminals stain
a bright blue against a reddish background. The effect is not
due to enzymatic changes but instead probably reflects an
increased affinity of degeneration products (or glia) for
iodine; the most telling bit of evidence for this conclusion
was the observation that only iodinated tetrazolium salts
produced the effect (Steward et al., 1973b). The complete
procedure is given in the two Steward et al., references cited
above and is reprinted at the end of this chapter (Figure 2).

The INT method has several features which might make it very
useful to psychobiologists. It is extremely simple and very
reliable. No fixatives are involved and only one incubation
step is needed. The method is also very fast since the
degeneration-specific staining is quite evident within hours
of the lesion. With this method lesions can be placed in the
morning and their results evaluated the same evening. On the
other hand the effect is still detectable many weeks after the
lesion. An investigator can therefore evaluate degeneration
at a survival time appropriate for his purposes, a point that
is obviously critical for behavioral studies.

Unfortunately, the technique also has several drawbacks. The
major reservation is that it cannot be used in fixed material.
This means that it must be carried out immediately after the
animal is sacrificed and more importantly, it is not appropriate
for high resolution examination. A second problem is the obvious
fact that this is a new method and there may be problems of an
unknown type associated with its use in certain systems. Finally,
the method undoubtedly has the axon-of-passage problem associated with it that was described above for the silver degeneration
technques.

But the simplicity of the method and the fact that it apparently
can be used at any time after the lesion indicates that an
investigator can test its appropriateness for his particular

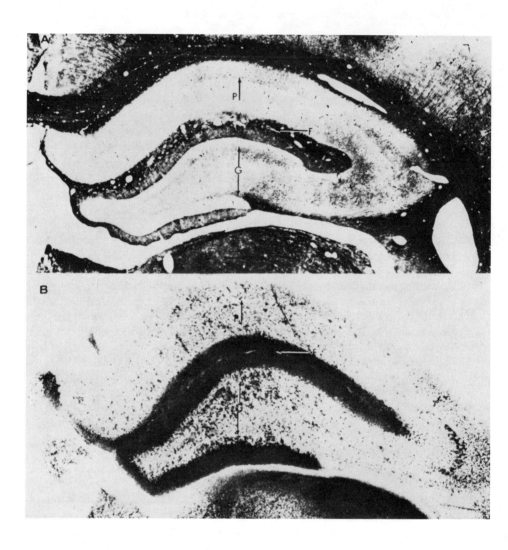

Fig. 2.   Comparison of zones of degeneration as revealed by
the Fink-Heimer technique (upper panel) and by the INT histochemical procedure described in the text (bottom panel). It is
apparent that there is almost perfect agreement between the two
methods. "P" indicates the pyramidal cell layer, "G" denotes
the granule cells of the dentate gyrus, while "F" marks the
hippocampal fissure (from Steward, Lynch and Cotman, 1973).

problem without a great expenditure of time. These features
of the INT procedure suggest that it may be of real value in
studies of brain-behavior relationships.

Acetylcholinesterase Histochemistry

Neuroanatomical systems often have particular biochemical
properties which are not shared by their neighbors. In some
cases it is possible to selectively stain these features and
thus visualize the system in question. Probably the best known
example of this approach to the anatomical analysis of the brain
is the recently evolved histofluorescent technique for demonstrating catecholamines and indoleamines. It is probably fair
to say that few technical developments have caused a more
profound change in our understanding of the anatomical
organization of the brain (cf. Fuxe and Ungerstad, 1966).
Unfortunately, the fluorescent methods require special equipment
and considerable skill and thus are not in their present form
appropriate for routine use in neurobehavioral studies.

There are other histochemical techniques however which can be
used quite readily in these types of experiments. Many neural
systems, including much of the limbic system, contain the
enzyme acetylcholinesterase (AChE). This enzyme can be easily
and selectively converted into a very evident brown or black
reaction product by a well known histochemical technique. The
procedure involves normal perfusion followed by a relatively
brief fixation period (1-2 days) and then sectioning and
development. Note also that alternate sections can be used for
Nissl stains. The technique included in the appendix is extremely reliable and can be easily performed in any laboratory
equipped with a freezing microtome and a fume hood. Figure 3
shows an example of the results which can be achieved with the
technique.

The method has several potential values for psychobiological
work. It is extremely helpful in delineating the nuclei and
subnuclei of the brain; many of the amygdaloid and thalamic
groups, for example, are much more obvious when stained for
AChE than when examined in Nissl stained preparations. In
some areas this is also true of the layers of paleo- and
neocortex (see Figure 3). The method could therefore be of
real help in describing the sites of lesions and the location
of stimulation electrodes.

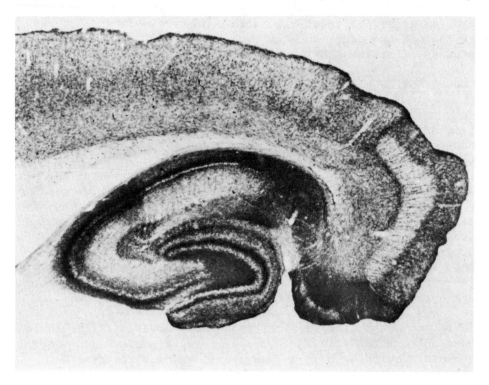

Fig. 3.   Horizontal section through the hippocampal formation
stained for acetylcholinesterase activity as described in the
text (from Mosko, Lynch and Cotman, 1973).

If the region under study does in fact contain high concentrations of the enzyme then a little further effort can provide
some very useful information about the connections of that
system. Specifically, it is possible to establish if the
AChE is contained in cell bodies or terminals in the region
in question; that is, if the region gives rise to an AChE
projection or is innervated by one. The organophosphorous
compound di-isopropylfluorophosphate (DFP) irreversibly inhibits
AChE activity. A systemic injection of this drug depletes
brain AChE activity, as shown by both biochemical and histochemical techniques. About 4 hours after the injection, staining

returns but is restricted to cell bodies presumably because
this is where new enzyme is being synthesized (cf. Lynch, Lucas
and Deadwyler, 1973). It is only several hours later that
neuropil staining returns. Therefore if a given brain region
contains AChE positive cells this can be easily established
by sacrificing the animal 4-6 hours after DFP injection. If
on the other hand the enzyme is contained in terminals arising
from a distant source then little AChE activity will be detected
at that time (see Lynch, Lucas and Deadwyler, 1973 for an
application of this strategy).

As shown in Figure 4 a goodly amount of cytological detail
is evident in the AChE-positive cells detected 4-6 hours after
DFP treatment. This makes it possible to relate these cells
to those revealed by the Golgi technique, a correlation that
can in many cases prove very valuable.

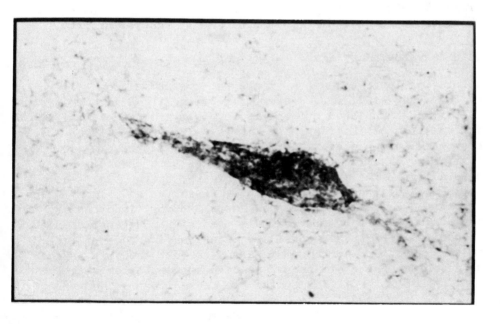

Fig. 4. Cell stained for AChE activity 4-6 hours after
systemic injection of DFP (from Lynch, Lucas and Deadwyler,
1973).

Having established that a given brain area gives rise to or is
innervated by a AChE positive projection, one can go a step
further and investigate the origins (or terminations) of these
projections. Lesions of AChE containing cell bodies causes a
loss of staining in the terminals of those cells within 48
hours. Therefore the projections of brain regions containing
AChE positive cells can be examined by making a lesion at that
site and searching for enzyme depletion in likely target regions.
This approach has been used with good results by Shute and
Lewis (1967).

In performing experiments of the type just discussed the
possibility of trans-synaptic loss of enzyme should be considered
Definitive evidence on the occurrence or non-occurrence of this
effect is not available but the possibility certainly cannot
be ignored. This is especially true of studies in which the
lesion was placed a considerable time prior to sacrifice.

Despite this reservation, AChE histochemistry offers a simple,
effective means of describing the cytoarchitecture and
connections of a particular type of brain system. Since many
brain systems studied by psychobiologists are AChE-containing
the strategies just described could be of general utility.

Autoradiographic methods

Autoradiographic techniques represent a genuine breakthrough
in the study of nervous system connections. The method involves
injecting a tritiated amino acid (usually proline or leucine)
into an area of interest where it is taken up by cell bodies,
converted into proteins and transported by axoplasmic flow to
terminals. The radioactive proteins are then demonstrated
autoradiographically, providing a picture of the "labelled"
cells and their axons and terminals (Lasak et al., 1968; Cowan
et al., 1972). This method possesses two very important
advantages over the more commonly used silver degeneration
procedures. First and foremost, axons passing through the
injection site do not accumulate and convert the tritiated
amino acids, therefore the axons-of-passage problem which
provides so much difficulty for the Fink-Heimer method (see
above) is obviated. Secondly, it is probable that the
technique is more sensitive than degeneration methods since

all neurons presumably incorporate amino acids and synthesize
proteins. (However, in view of the recent development of AR
as a routine method it is not possible to provide any firm
statements about its relative sensitivity across species and
brain systems).

A drawback to the AR method for neurobehavioral work lies in
its comparative difficulty. The method involves several steps
which require some practice and considerable time. There are
many sources of error in the method and some specialized
facilities are required (e.g., a darkroom). Therefore this
technique in its current form would require some commitment
of resources and personnel by any worker intending to use it
routinely in a neurobehavioral program. The interested reader
is referred to the recent comprehensive review by Cowan et al.,
1972 for further details and protocols.

Horseradish peroxidase histochemistry

A second recently developed transport technique makes use of
the enzyme horseradish peroxidase (HRP). This compound has been
used for years to study uptake and transport mechanisms in
peripheral tissue and recently it has been found that the cell
bodies (Lynch, et al., 1973a, 1974) and terminals of neurons
also take it up (Kristensson and Olsson, 1971; LaVail and
LaVail, 1972). The enzyme is then transported in both orthograde (from cells towards terminals) and retrograde directions
(from terminals to cells) after which it can be demonstrated
histochemically. HRP can be used therefore to locate the cell
bodies which give rise to a population of terminals or to follow
the projections of a given collections of neurons (Fig. 5).

This method possesses a number of very exciting features. As
a retrograde method it could resolve a number of long-standing
anatomical problems; it is at least conceivable that a single
injection might reveal all the brain regions which innervate
the site of application. As an orthograde technique, it is
far simpler and much more rapid than autoradiography and
involves no specialized equipment. In addition, horseradish
peroxidase can be ejected from micropipettes and used to
impregnate neurons in a Golgi like fashion. Using this
technique it is possible to selectively impregnate small groups
of cells in any given neural structure (Killackey, Dunwiddie

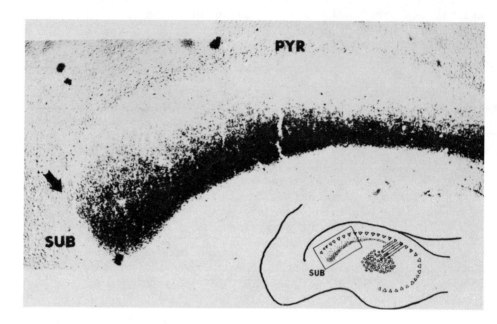

Fig. 5.   The results of an experiment in which a large injecti
of horseradish peroxidase was made into the regio inferior of th
hippocampus.   The photomicrograph shows the densely labelled
terminals of the Schaffer collateral system in the regio superio
The insert shows the site of the injection (stripes) and the
location of the labelled terminals (dots) "SUB" indicates the
subiculum, "PYR" marks the layer of pyramidal cell bodies of the
regio superior (from Lynch, Gall, Mensah and Cotman, 1974).

and Lynch, 1974).   Further, this technique can also be used
in conjunction with electrophysiological recording methods in
order to extracellularly label individual neurons in the
region of the electrode tip using microiontophoresis (Lynch,
Gall and Deadwyler, 1974).   A final advantage is that the
HRP histochemical reaction product can be made electron dense
thereby providing an opportunity for correlating light
microscopic study of cells or their elements with ultra-
structural analysis of those same elements.

Despite its simplicity there are several problems with the HRP method which may restrict its general usage. The major reservation is that the enzyme apparently does not reach the terminals of all axonal projections; thus the technique will be much more informative in some systems than others. The reasons for this limitation are obscure but may relate to the distance between the injection and the terminals or the transport characteristics of certain cell types. Similarly, we suspect that in some cases retrograde transport of the enzyme does not reach all the cells whose axons innervate a given site. Hopefully, future research will rectify these problems but currently negative results with HRP histochemistry (either as an orthograde or retrograde method) will have to be interpreted with a great deal of caution.

A second point that needs to be emphasized regarding this technique is that the benzidene compounds used to develop the enzyme are carcinogenic and must be handled with a great deal of care. A fume hood, disposable glassware and considerable caution are absolutely necessary.

The present discussion has focused on a number of the newer anatomical techniques, most of which can be employed by the nominally equipped laboratory. It is our belief that to fully understand the nervous system neuroanatomical techniques such as these are going to have to be combined with physiological and behavioral techniques for the multifaceted complexity of the nervous system does not reveal itself from any single angle.

APPENDIX I

The Fink-Heimer Stain as used in this laboratory.

I. Specimens

The animal is first perfused transcardially with normal
saline followed by 10% formalin. The brain is then carefully
removed and stored in 10% formalin for several days. The
brain is then transferred to sugar formalin (35 gms table
sugar/100 ML 10% formalin) and stored for a week or until
brain sinks. This procedure prevents the formation of ice
crystals during frozen sectioning. Section brain on freezing
microtome at 30 to 50 microns. Store sections in 2% formalin
until ready to stain.

II. Equipment

Glassware, timer, 12 compartment ice cube trays which hold 25
to 30 ML per compartment (available from Sears & Roebuck, Inc
or local hardware store), perforated coors crucibles No. 7 (to
fit in ice tray compartments), agitator to hold and moderately
agitate several ice cube trays (Any type will do. Our present
agitator is a modified used reducing machine costing fifteen
dollars).

III. Solutions

(Numbered according to step in which they are used)

2. .05% $KMnO_4$
3. Bleach: Equal parts 1% oxalic acid and freshly made
    1% hydroquinone.
5. Fink I solution: 1 gram uranyl nitrate and 5 grams
    silver nitrate in 1 liter double distilled water
7. Ammonical silver: 10 ML 2.5% silver nitrate to
    1 ML combined NH_4OH and 2.5% NaOH (ratio of NH_4OH
    to 2.5% NaOH either 6 parts to 9 parts, 1:1
    or 9:6 as determined by trial procedure outlined
    below).
9. Reducer: 75 ML 95% EtOH, 20 ML 1% citric acid, 18
    ML 10% formalin to 1800 ML double distilled water
    (additional 1% citric acid may be added as determined
    by trial procedure below).
11. Hypo: 1% sodium thiosulfate

IV. Procedure

(For steps 1-7 inclusive place trays on agitator, each crucible
can hold several sections)

1. Double distilled H_2O 3 changes (first 10 minutes,
    (2nd and 3rd 3 min. each).
2. $KMNO_4$ (10 minutes).
3. Bleach (1 minute).
4. Double distilled H_2O 3 changes (3 min. each).
5. Fink I solution (overnight or approx. 16 hours).
6. Double distilled H_2O 3 changes (1st 2 minutes 2nd
    and 3rd 1 minute each.
7. Ammonical silver (2 minutes).
8. Blot crucibles well on paper towels.
9. Reducer 3 changes (1 minute total time in reducer).
10. Double distilled water 2 changes (2 minutes each).
11. Hypo (1 minute).
12. Double distilled H_2O 3 changes (first two 2 minutes
    each; leave in third until mounted).
13. Mount sections on to slides from alcoholic gelatin
    (.5 GMS gelatin dissolved in 100 ML distilled H_2O
    filtered and combined with 100 ML 80% EtOH made
    fresh each week).
14. Place in 95% EtOH until all sections are mounted.
15. Dehydrate in two changes absolute EtOH (4 min each).
16. Clear in toluene 4 changes (3 minutes each).
17. Coverslip with permount.
18. Clean all glassware, trays and crucibles with hot
    soapy water, rinse, soak for at least 1/2 hour in
    5% nitric acid, rinse in double distilled water and
    dry (very important if consistent results are to be
    obtained).

V. Trials Procedure

(To obtain optimal impregnation)

The procedure is essentially the same except only one section
is placed in each crucible and only twelve sections are stained.
The sections used should be from the area of the lesions so that
the experimenter is reasonably sure degenerative debris will
be present. The only changes in the procedure are in steps
7 and 9).

7. <u>Ammonical silver</u>

The first four compartments are filled with 2.5%
silver nitrate and a mixture of ammonium hydroxide
and sodium hydroxide in the ratio of 9 parts NH_4OH
to six parts NaOH (for example, 45 ML 2.5% silver
nitrate plus 2.7 ML conc. NH_4OH and 1.8 ML 2.5 NaOH).
For the second four trays the ratio of ammonium
hyroxide to sodium hyroxide is one to one. For the
third four compartments the ratio is 6 parts NH_4OH
to 9 parts NaOH.

9. <u>Reducer</u>

Take four beakers containing 100 ML each of reducer
prepared as above. The first beaker is used as is in
compartments 1, 5 & 9 in all three reducer changes.
To the second beaker add 1/4 ML additional 1% citric
acid, use in compartments 2, 6 and 10. To the third
beaker add 1/2 ML additional 1% citric acid, use in
compartments 3, 7 and 11. To the remaining beaker
add 1 ML additional 1% citric acid, use in compartments of 4, 8 and 12.

For this procedure it is of course necessary to keep
track of what solutions have been used in each
compartment. The trials procedure results in twelve
uniquely stained sections from which the best
impregnation can be chosen to be employed for the
entire case.

APPENDIX II

<u>Iodonitrotetrazolium violet (INT) histochemistry</u>
(from Steward, Cotman and Lynch, 1973)

1) Lesion animal.
2) Sacrifice 8-24 hours later.
3) Remove brain and section immediately with freezing
   microtome at 50 - 75 um.
4) Transfer sections to incubation medium consisting of:
   0.1 M Tris buffer (pH 7.4).
   75 mM sodium succinate
   1 mM INT (Sigma Chemical Co).
5) Incubate for 15 minutes.
6) Mount on slides and cover with glycerol jelly.
   (Humanson, 1967).

APPENDIX III

Acetylcholinesterase Histochemical Technique for the Light
Microscope (Modified from Koelle, 1949).

Fixation
1.   Perfuse intracardially with 10% formalin-saline
2.   Store in perfusate at $4^{\circ}C$ for no longer than 3 days.

Reagents
1.   Solution A: 3.75 gm glycine
                   1.6 gm anhydrous cupric sulphate
                   (or 2.5 gm $CuSO_4$. $5H_2O$)
                   100 ml Distilled H_2O
2.   0.1 M $CuSO_4$
3.   0.1N acetate-acetic acid buffer, pH 5.3
4.   Acetylthiocholine Iodide
5.   Promethazine
6.   1% ammonium sulfide
     Reagents 1, 2 and 3 may be kept as stock solutions at
     $4^{\circ}C$. Reagents 4 and 5 should be kept frozen.

Procedure
1.   Prepare solution B by combining the following
     ingredients, in order, in a centrifuge tube
     3 ml distilled water
     1 ml 0.1m $CuSO_4$
     58 mg Acetylthiocholine iodide
2.   Spin down precipitate for 10 minutes
3.   Prepare the incubation solution by combining the
     following ingredients:
     20 ml 0.1M acetate-acetic acid buffer, pH 5.3
     14 ml distilled water
     0.8 ml 8.8 mM promethazine
     1.6 ml solution A
     Solution B: Supernatant from step 2.
4.   Slice 25 - 40 micron sections on freezing microtome
     Place sections directly into incubation solution.
5.   Incubate sections overnight
6.   Develop sections in 1% ammonium sulfide under a
     fume hood. (Transfer sections individually from the
     incubation solution directly to the ammonium sulfide
     solution. Sections should have attained the appropriate
     color within approximately 45 seconds).

7. Rinse in distilled water for 15 seconds.
8. Immediately mount each section onto albumin coated slide from a water wash.
9. Let air dry at least 6 hours.
10. Butyl alcohol 10 minutes.
11. Xylene - 10 minutes.
12. Cover slip using permount.

Notes:

Promethazine is an inhibitor of non-specific cholinesterases, and may be omitted.

The incubation time may be varied widely to produce the desired staining intensity with longer incubation times producing darker staining.

APPENDIX IV

Horseradish Peroxidase Histochemical Technique for the Light Microscope (Modified from Lynch et al., 1974)

Fixation
1. Perfusion
   a. 0.9% saline
   b. 10% formalin-saline
2. Store in perfusion solution (b) for 18 hours at 4°C. The addition of DMSO at a 10% concentration to this storage solution seems to improve the quality of the sections without inhibiting the peroxidase reaction product.

Reagents
1. 2% Benzidine Dihydrochloride in 30% EtOH
2. 0.06% Hydrogen Peroxide
3. 6% Sodium Nitroprusside in 50% EtOH
   Reagents 1 and 3 may be kept as stock solutions at 4°C. Reagent 2 should be mixed fresh from a 3% stock solution kept at 4°C.

Procedure
1. Slice 35 micron sections on freezing microtome. Place sections directly into cold 30% sucrose. Sections may be developed immediately or stored in the sucrose solution at 4°C overnight.

2. Wash sections in distilled water at 0°C for 5-15 min.
3. Rinse in 25% EtOH at 0°C for 15-30 sec.
4. Incubate for approximately 1 min. at 0°C in a fresh solution containing 10 ml of the Benzidine solution and 10 ml of the Hydrogen Peroxide solution.
5. Wash sections <u>briefly</u> in 35% EtOH at 0°C.
6. Stabilize in Nitroprusside solution for 15 min. at 0°C.
7. Wash sections briefly in 25% EtOH at 0°C.
8. Immediately mount sections onto albumin-coated slides from a water wash.
9. Let air dry
10. Counterstain with Safranin O.

References

Benevento, L.A. and Ebner, F.F.   The areas and layers of corticocortical terminations in the visual cortex of the Virginia opossum. J. Comp. Neurol., 1971, 141, 157-190.

Clarke, E. and O'Malley, C.D.   The Human Brain and Spinal Cord. Univ. of Calif. Press Berkeley, 1968.

Cowan, W.M., Gottlieb, D.I., Hendrickson, A., Price, J.L. and Woolsey, T.A.   The autoradiographic demonstration of axonal connections in the central nervous system. Brain Res., 1972, 37, 21-51.

Fink, R.P. and Heimer, L.   Two methods for selective silver impregnation of degenerating axons and their synaptic ends in the central nervous system. Brain Res., 1967, 4, 369-374.

Fuxe, K. and Ungerstadt, U.   Fluorescent microscopy in neuro-anatomy. S. Ebbessen and W. Nauta, (Eds.). Contemporary Research in Neuroanatomy, Springer, New York, 1970, pp. 275-314.

Guillery, R.W.   Light- and electron-microscopical studies of normal and degenerating axons. S. Ebbessen and W. Nauta, (Eds.). Contemporary Research in Neuroanatomy, Springer, New York, 1970, pp. 77-105.

Hand, D.J. and Morrison, A.R.   Thalmocortical relationships in
    the somatic sensory system as revealed by silver
    impregnation techniques. Brain, Behav. Evol., 1972
    5, 273-302.

Heimer, L.   Selective silver impregnation of degenerating
    axoplasm. S. Ebbessen and W. Nauta, (Eds.). Contemporary
    Research in Neuroanatomy, Springer, New York, 1970, pp.
    106-131.

Heimer, L.   Bridging the gap between light and electron
    microscopy in the experimental tracing of fiber connections.
    S. Ebbessen and W. Nauta, (Eds.). Contemporary Research in
    Neuroanatomy, Springer, New York, 1970, pp. 162-172

Humanson, G.L.   Animal tissue techniques. Freeman, San
    Francisco, 1967. pp. 130.

Kalil, R.E.   Formation of new retino-geniculate connections
    in kittens after removal of one eye. Anat. Rec., 1972,
    172, 339-340.

Killackey, H.   Projections of the ventral nucleus to neocortex
    in the hedgehog. Anat. Rec., 1972, 172, 345.

Killackey, H. and Ebner, F.F.   Two different types of thalmo-
    cortical projections to a single cortical area in mammals.
    Brain, Behav. Evol., 1972, 6, 141-169.

Killackey, H.   Anatomical evidence for cortical subdivisions
    based on vertically discrete thalamic projections from the
    ventral posterior nucleus to cortical barrels in the rat.
    Brain Res., 1973, 51, 326-331.

Killackey, H. and Ebner, F.F.   Convergent projection of three
    separate thalamic nuclei on to a single cortical area.
    Science, 1973, 179, 283-285.

Killackey, H., Lynch, G. and Dunwiddie, T.   Extracellular
    labelling of neurons in somatic sensory cortex with
    horseradish peroxidase. Anat. Rec., 1974, 178, 390-391.

Kristensson, K. and Olsson, Y.   Retrograde axonal transport of
    protein. Brain Res., 1971, 29, 363-365.

LaVail, J.H. and LaVail, M.M.   Retrograde axonal transport in
    the central nervous system, Science, 1972, 176, 1416-1417.

Lasek, R., Joseph, B.S. and Whitlock, D.G.   Evaluation of a
    radioautographic neuroanatomical tracing method. Brain Res.,
    1968, 8, 319-336.

Lewis, P.R. and Shute, C.C.D.   The cholinergic limbic system:
    Projection to hippocampal formation, medial cortex, nuclei
    of the ascending cholinergic reticular system and the
    subfornical organ and supra-optic crest. Brain, 1967, 90,
    521-537.

Lund, R.D. and Lund, J.S.   Reorganization of the retinotectal
    pathway in rats after neonatal retinal lesions. Exp. Neurol.,
    1973, 40, 337-390.

Lynch, G., Lucas, P. and Deadwyler, S.   The demonstration of
    acetylcholinesterase containing neurones within the caudate
    nucleus of the rat. Brain Res., 1972, 45, 617-621.

Lynch, G. Matthews, D., Mosko, S., Parks, T. and Cotman, C.W.
    Induced acetylcholinesterase-rich layer in rat dentate gyrus
    following entorhinal lesions. Brain Res., 1972, 42, 311-
    318.

Lynch, G., Smith, R.L., Mensah, P. and Cotman, C.W.   Tracing
    the dentate gyrus mossy fiber system with horseradish
    peroxidase histochemistry. Exp. Neurol., 1973, 40, 516-
    524.

Lynch, G., Stanfield, B. and Cotman, C.W.   Developmental
    differences in post-lesion axonal growth in the hippocampus.
    Brain Res., 1973, 59, 155-168.

Lynch, G., Mosko, S., Parks, T. and Cotman, C.W.   Relocation
    and hyperdevelopment of the dentate gyrus commissural system
    after entorhinal lesions in immature rats. Brain Res., 1973,
    50, 174-178.

Lynch, G., Gall, C., Mensah, P. and Cotman, C.W.   Horseradish
    peroxidase histochemistry: A new method for tracing
    efferent projections in the central nervous system. Brain
    Res., 1974, 65, 373-380.

Lynch, G., Deadwyler, S.A. and Gall, C.   Labeling of central
    nervous system neurones with extracellular recording
    microelectrodes. Brain Res., 1974, 66, 337-341.

Mosko, S., Lynch, G. and Cotman, C.W.   Distribution of the
    septal projection to the hippocampal formation of the rat.
    J. Comp. Neurol., 1973, 152, 163-174.

Melgren, S.I. and Blackstad, T.W.   Oxidative enzymes (tetrazoli-
    um reductases) in the hippocampal region of the rat, distri-
    bution and relation to architectonics. Z. Zellforsch., 1967
    78, 167-207.

Nauta, W.J.H. and Ryan, L.F.   Selective silver impregnation of
    degenerating axons in the central nervous system. Stain
    Technol., 1952, 27, 175-179.

Nauta, H.J.W. and Gygax, P.A.   Silver impregnation of
    degenerating axons in the central nervous system: A
    modified technique. Stain Technol., 1954, 29, 91-93.

Schneider, G.E.   Mechanisms of functional recovery following
    lesions of visual cortex or superior colliculus in neonate
    and adult hamsters. Brain, Behav. Evol., 1970 , 3, 295-
    323.

Shute, C.C.D. and Lewis, P.R.   The use of cholinesterase
    techniques combined with operative procedures to follow
    nervous pathways in the brain.   In H.G. Schwarzacher (Ed.).
    Biblio, Anatomica, F.2 - Histochemsitry of Cholinesterase.
    Karger, New York, 1961, 34-39.

Siegel, A., Bandler, R. and Flynn, J.P.   Thalamic sites and
    pathways related to elicited attack. Brain, Behav. Evol.,
    1972, 6, 542-555.

Steward, O., Cotman, C.W. and Lynch, G.   The nature of increased
    histochemical deposition of INT formazan in fields of
    degenerating synaptic terminals. Brain Res., 1973, 63,
    183-193.

Steward, O., Lynch, G. and Cotman, C.   Histochemical detection
    of orthograde degeneration in the central nervous system of
    the rat. Brain Res., 1973, 54, 65-73.

Steward, O., Cotman, C.W. and Lynch, G.   Growth of a new fiber
      projection in the brain of adult rats: Re-innervation of
      the dentate gyrus by the contralateral entorhinal cortex
      following ipsilateral entorhinal lesions. Exp. Brain Res.,
      In press.

Strick, P.O.   Cortical projections of the feline thalamic
      nucleus ventralis lateralus. Brain Res., 1970, 20,
      130-134.

PHYSIOLOGICAL AND PHARMACOLOGICAL ANALYSIS OF BEHAVIOR

John A. Harvey

Department of Psychology

University of Iowa

Iowa City, Iowa 52242

Psychologists have traditionally employed ablation techniques, electrical stimulation, and parenteral or central administration of drugs to examine subsequent effects on behavior. The problems that have arisen with the use of these techniques are described below. However, the one basic problem has been our inability to specify the exact mechanisms by which these procedures exert their effects on behavior. For example the ablation technique is one of the oldest and most extensively used methods for studying brain function. Consequently, we know a great deal about the behavioral changes produced by a variety of cortical and subcortical lesions. However, in most cases we do not know how to interpret the results. First, in almost all cases the lesion is simply described by the primary locus of damage. Rarely does the investigator examine the degeneration occurring outside of this primary locus. Consequently, the anatomical system being affected by a lesion is unknown. More importantly, the ablation technique as employed for study of brain function has not allowed us to specify the mechanism(s) by which lesions produce

a change in function. This is due to the fact that replacement
of the brain tissue destroyed, either by transplantation or by
injection of an extract of that tissue, has not been possible.

If one removes the adrenal cortex, one can see a variety of
effects. One can, however, determine to what extent these
effects are reversible by either transplanting adrenal cortex or
by injection of adrenocortical extracts. In this way we have
discovered the role of various adrenal hormones and of ACTH as
well as the function and mechanism by which the adrenal cortex
exerts its control over a variety of processes. We also realize
that the effects produced by adrenalectomy are not due to the
removal of tissue per se, but rather to changes at distant
target sites upon which adrenocortical hormones normally act.

In contrast to this approach, it is usually assumed, at least
implicitly, that the behavioral effects of brain lesions can be
ascribed to the absence of tissue per se. This presupposes that
the remaining portions of the brain have not been altered by
the lesion, an assumption that has now been proven false. For
example, we now know that lesions can induce morphological
changes in brain through axonal sprouting which may lead to new
functional connections in brain (see Lynch this volume). As a
result, the views of Jackson (1898) that the effects of a lesion
are due to a reorganization of the remaining areas of the brain
rather than to the tissue destroyed; Von Manakow's theory of
diaschesis (1911); and Cannon's theory of central denervation
supersensitivity (Cannon and Rosenbleuth, 1949) still remain
tenable. Such theories also can more easily account for recovery
of function after brain damage.

Similar criticisms can be applied to the other methods for
studying brain function. Electrical stimulation of the brain
has often been used without a knowledge of the anatomical systems
being affected, since it has been difficult to specify the
exact pathways whose stimulation is mediating the behavioral
responses. The effects of central or peripheral administration
of drugs are often interpreted on the basis of their presumed
actions in the periphery, actions which do not necessarily occur
centrally.

Although we have long known that each neuron in the brain
synthesizes a specific synaptic transmitter which is released
when the neuron fires, we have not been able to identify these
transmitters with complete certainty. This has been the major

stumbling block in our ability to specify the mechanisms by which lesions, electrical stimulation, or drugs act on the brain. In the autonomic nervous sytem we know that stimulation of the preganglionic fibers leads to certain effects because such stimulation releases acetylcholine (ACh) at the ganglion, and that ACh is the synaptic transmitter which in turn leads to depolarization and firing of the postganglionic neurons. If we have any doubts about this, we need simply block the ganglionic action of ACh with a specific drug. Similarly, we know that changes produced by destruction of the cholinergic-preganglionic fibers are due to the subsequent degeneration of the terminals innervating the ganglion and the loss of ACh. Any doubts about this can be tested by showing that application of ACh to the denervated ganglion leads to a firing of the postganglionic fibers. Similarly, because of our knowledge of the transmitters involved, we know in most cases how various drugs produce changes in the functioning of the autonomic nervous system. Thus, in these instances we know the anatomy and chemistry by which certain effects of drugs, lesions, or stimulation are obtained.

Within the past 20 years, a similar knowledge of the brain has been slowly developing. First of all, a number of compounds have been identified as putative synaptic transmitters in the central nervous system. A partial list of these would include: ACh; serotonin (5-HT); norepinephrine (NE); dopamine (DA); γ-amino butyric acid (GABA); glycine; aspartate; glutamate; proline; adenosine; and substance P. Secondly, within the past 10 years we have discovered that many of these transmitters are anatomically distributed in specific nuclei and fiber tracts. Finally, it has been demonstrated that certain drugs as well as lesions or electrical stimulation of specific brain sites can produce changes in the brain content or turnover of these compounds. These findings force us to alter our views concerning the manner by which brain lesions or electrical stimulation produce changes in behavior, and thus provide us with new insights into these old experimental tools. This paper will summarize data suggesting that drugs, lesions, and electrical stimulation produce effects on behavior by a common mechanism, which involves changes in specific chemical systems in the brain.

CENTRAL PATHWAYS FOR PUTATIVE SYNATPIC TRANSMITTERS

The first demonstration that a putative synaptic transmitter was associated with a specific fiber system in brain came from ablation studies in the rat. These studies (text continued on p. 132)

A. NORADRENERGIC PATHWAYS

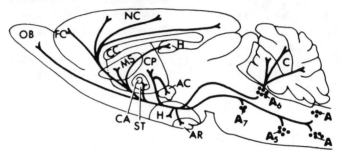

B. DOPAMINERGIC PATHWAYS

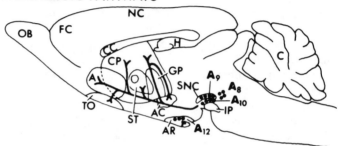

C. SEROTONERGIC PATHWAYS

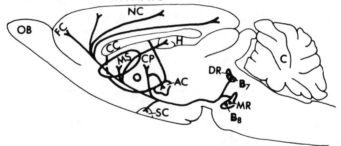

D. CHOLINERGIC PATHWAYS

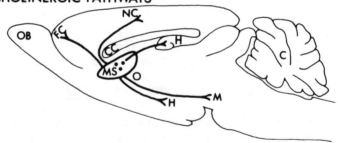

Figure 1

FIGURE 1

Abbreviations used in text figure:

A	Accumbens nucleus
AC	Central amygdaloid nucleus
AR	Arcuate nucleus
C	Cerebellum
CA	Anterior commissure
CC	Corpus Callosum
CP	Caudate-putamen
DR	Dorsal raphe nucleus
FC	Frontal cortex
GP	Globus pallidus
H	Hypothalamus
HIP	Hippocampus
IP	Interpeduncular nucleus
M	Mesencephalon
MR	Median raphe nucleus
MS	Medial septal nucleus
NC	Neocortex
OB	Olfactory bulb
SC	Suprachiasmatic nucleus
SNC	Substantia nigra, pars compacta
ST	Interstitial nucleus of the stria terminalis
TO	Olfactory tubercle

Schematic representation of the major pathways of putative
synaptic transmitters in brain. Black dots represent the location
of cell bodies and solid lines the pathways. Cell bodies are
numbered according to Dahlström and Fuxe (1964), the letter A
indicating catecholamine and the letter B serotonin cell bodies.

Figure 1A. Noradrenergic pathway[a]
   1. Dorsal Pathway: From cells located primarily in locus
coeruleus (A-6) via ventral tegmentum and medial forebrain bundle
and innervating: cerebellum, geniculate bodies, thalamic nuclei,
hypothalamus (sparse), and entire telencephalon including septum,
caudate-putamen, amygdala, hippocampus, cingulate cortex and
entire neocortex.

---

[a]Dahlström and Fuxe, 1964; Ungerstedt, 1971a

2. Ventral Pathway: From cells located primarily in
medulla oblongata and Pons (cell groups A-1, A-2, A-5, A-7) via
the ventral tegmentum and medial forebrain bundle and innervating:
the brain stem especially hypothalamic structures such as nucleus
dorsalis medialis, nucleus periventricularis, area ventral to the
fornix, arcuate nucleus, interstitial layer of median eminence,
retro-chiasmatic area, nucleus paraventricularis, nucleus
supraopticus as well as the preoptic area and the interstitial
nucleus of the stria terminalis, ventral part.

Figure 1B. Dopaminergic Pathway[b]
1. Nigrostriatal Bundle: From cells located in the pars
compacta of the substantia nigra (A-9) and in the ventral
tegmentum (A-8) via the ventral tegmentum, medial forebrain
bundle, internal capsule, and globus pallidus to the caudate-
putamen, and amygdala.
2. Meso-limbic Pathway: From cells located dorsal to the
interpenducular nucleus (A-10) via the ventral tegmentum and
medial forebrain bundle to the accumbens nucleus, interstitial
nucleus of the stria terminalis, dorsal part, and olfactory
tubercle.
3. Tubero-infundibular Pathway: From cells in arcuate
nucleus (A-12) to the external layer of the median eminence.

Figure 1C. Serotonergic Pathway[c]
1. Forebrain Pathway: From cells located in the dorsal and
median raphe nuclei (B-7 and B-8) via the ventral tegmentum and
medial forebrain bundle and innervating: suprachiasmatic nucleus
and entire telencephalon including septum, caudate-putamen,
amygdala, hippocampus, cingulate cortex and entire neocortex.
2. Cerebellar Pathway: From raphe cells in metencephalon
(B-5 and B-6) to cerebellum.

Figure 1D. Cholinergic Pathway[d]
1. Dorsal Tegmental Pathway: From cells located in nucleus
cuniformis to tectum and thalamus.

---

[b]Ungerstedt, 1971a

[c]Heller, Harvey and Moore, 1962; Dahlström and Fuxe, 1964;
Ungerstedt, 1971a.

[d]Shute and Lewis, 1967; Lewis and Shute, 1967; Pepeu, Mulas,
Ruffi and Sotgiu, 1971; Sorensen and Harvey, 1971. The dorsal
and ventral tegmental pathways have not been verified and so are
not shown in the figure.

2.   Ventral Tegmental Pathway: From cells located in ventral tegmental area and substantia nigra to subthalamus, hypothalamus and basal forebrain areas.

3.   Septal Projections: From cells in medial septal nuclei to the hippocampus and from cells within the septal area (origin not certain) to cerebral cortex, hypothalamus, and mesencephalon.

demonstrate that destruction of the medial forebrain bundle (MFB)
or of areas associated with this fiber system (dorso-medial midbrain tegmentum, ventral midbrain tegmentum, and septal area)
significantly decreased brain content of 5-HT. This effect of the
lesions followed a time course compatible with the time required
for the degeneration of small nonmyelinated fibers (Heller, et al.,
1962; Harvey, et al., 1963). These data suggested the existence
of a serotonergic pathway in brain that followed the distribution
of the MFB. Subsequently, lesion studies also demonstrated
the existence of a noradrenergic (Heller and Harvey, 1963) and a
dopaminergic (Andén, et al., 1964) pathway in brain.

The application of the histochemical method of Falck and Hillarp
(1959) led to the mapping of these monoaminergic fiber systems
(Dahlström and Fuxe, 1964; Ungerstedt, 1971a). The pathways
that have been described so far are presented in Figure 1. These
neural systems are quite analogous to the peripheral autonomic
nervous system, in that they constitute a chemically identifiable
series of distinct fiber systems originating from discrete groups
of cells in the brain stem and innervating specific diencephalic
and telencephalic structures. As is evident from Figure 1,
lesions can be placed so as to produce a loss of one or more of
these transmitter systems. The effectiveness of the lesion can
be assessed qualitatively by examining the loss of fluorescent
terminals in various brain regions or quantitatively by measuring
the decrease in monoamine content by chemical analysis (Table 1).

The decreases in monoamine content occur primarily in the
telencephalon since the majority of axon terminals, the portion
of the neuron which contains the highest content of transmitter,
are located in telencephalic structures. This is especially
true of lesions placed in the more rostral portions of the
ascending monoaminergic pathways, as for example, the MFB, since
such lesions do not affect the diencephalic projections to as
great an extent as do lesions within the nuclear groups in the
brain stem. As a consequence of these anatomical arrangements,
lesions in the raphe nuclei can produce decreases of 80% or more
in the telencephalic content of 5-HT without affecting content
of NE or DA. Lesions in the locus coeruleus will produce
decreases of approximately 70% in telencephalic content of NE
without affecting 5-HT or DA. Lesions placed in the MFB, the
point of convergence of all three ascending monoaminergic
pathways, will produce significant decreases in the telencephalic
content of 5-HT, DA and NE (Table 1).

TABLE I

Effect of Lesions on Brain Content of Putative Synaptic Transmitters

Brain Lesion	Brain Region	% Decrease From Control			
		5-HT	NE	DA	ACh
Raphe Nuclei	Telencephalon	-82*	- 7	+ 2	--
Locus Coeruleus	Telencephalon	- 9	-73*	+ 7	--
Nigro Striatal Bundle	Telencephalon	-45*	-46*	-75*	0
Medial Forebrain Bundle	Telencephalon	-77*	-28*	-74*	- 4*
Septal Area	Telencephalon	-22*	-12	+ 6	-37*
	Diencephalon & Rostral-Midbrain	--	--	--	-20*
	Hippocampus	--	--	--	-75*

Data taken from: Simpson, Grabarits, and Harvey, 1967; Harvey, Schlosberg, and Yunger, 1974; Green and Harvey, 1974; Pepeu, et al., 1971; and Kuhar, et al., 1973.

*Indicates a decrease significantly different from control (p<0.05).

The decrease in monoamine content following lesions appears to be due to the degeneration of the axon terminals since one can detect the degenerative changes by electron microscopy (Aghajanian, et al., 1969) or by histochemical fluorescence methods (Ungerstedt, 1971a). In addition, one sees parallel decreases in monoamine content, activity of the synthetic enzymes (tryptophan-5-hydroxylase and tyrosine hydroxylase), and uptake of the monoamines by synaptosomal fractions of various telencephalic areas (Zigmond, et al., 1971; Kuhar, et al., 1972). The measurement of these chemical changes following a lesion provides the most sensitive method for assessing degenerative changes since current silver stains do not appear to always detect terminal degeneration of such small fibers (Ungerstedt, 1971a; Hedreen and Chalmers, 1972). For this reason the existence of these pathways, as for example the projections from raphe neurons to neocortex including visual cortex, had not been previously detected by the standard histological techniques (see Lynch, this volume). Histochemical staining for acetylcholinesterase has led to a description of possible cholinergic pathways in brain (Shute and Lewis, 1967; Lewis and Shute, 1967). Since the occurrence of

acetylcholinesterase in a neuron does not necessarily imply the
existence of ACh, these maps must be viewed as pioneering
first steps. Corroboration requires the demonstration that
interruption of these pathways results in a decrease of ACh
content of areas they innervate. Such a corroboration has
recently been provided for the cholinergic projections from the
septum proposed by Lewis and Shute (1967). Lesions in the septal
area have been found to produce significant decreases of
approximately 20% in whole brain content of ACh (Pepeu, Mulas,
Ruffi and Sotgiu, 1971: Sorensen and Harvey, 1971). The decrease
occur in telencephalon, as well as in diencephalon and the rostra
portions of the mesencephalon (Table 1). These results demonstrate that a significant portion of the ACh content of brain is
regulated by a fiber system originating in or passing through
the septal area (Figure 1). The septo-hippocampal projections
proposed by Shute and Lewis (1967) have also been confirmed since
septal lesions produce a large (75%) decrease in hippocampal
content of ACh (Kuhar, et al., 1973; Pepeu, et al., 1973) (Table
1). The decrease in ACh content is paralleled by a decrease in
choline acetyltransferase activity and uptake of choline by
synaptosomal fractions obtained from hippocampus (Kuhar, et al.,
1973; see also Lynch, this volume).
It should be clear that the diagrams shown in Figure 1, represent
only the beginning of a thorough anatomical description of
various chemical pathways in the brain. Although the caudate
nucleus has the richest innervation by catecholaminergic neurons
(primarily dopaminergic) of any area in brain, this innervation
accounts for only about 15% of the axon terminals in the caudate
nucleus (Hökfelt, 1970). Various estimates for serotonin and
acetylcholine indicate that their terminals represent less than
10% of the total population within any given brain area (Snyder,
et al., 1973). Thus, there are a number of additional chemical
systems that will have to be discovered. For example, it has
recently been suggested that carnosine may be the synaptic
transmitter of olfactory nerve (Margolis, 1974), while aspartate
and glutamate may play a role in the olfactory tract (Harvey,
et al., 1974). Evidence for the role of amino acids has been
summarized recently by Synder, et al. (1973).

BRAIN LESIONS AS CHEMICAL MANIPULATIONS

The findings described above provide a new approach to the study
of brain function. Brain lesions can now be described not only
in terms of their morphological effects, but also in terms of

their chemical consequences. It is possible to examine whether
a particular behavioral effect of a lesion is due to the loss of
a specific synaptic transmitter in certain areas of brain. This
approach has been employed in our laboratory for several years
and has allowed us to demonstrate that lesions having a common
effect of interrupting the serotonergic system and thus decreasing
telencephalic content of 5-HT also produce a common behavioral
effect, an increased sensitivity to painful stimuli (Harvey and
Lints, 1965; 1971). Such a chemical interpretation of a lesion
effect allows one to conduct control experiments not previously
possible. For example, one can mimic the effects of a lesion in
normal animals by the use of appropriate drugs. Animals injected
with p-chlorophenylalanine (p-CP) which inhibits brain tryptophan-
5-hydroxylase and thus depletes the brain of serotonin, also
produces an increased sensitivity to painful stimuli (Table 2).
Injection of 5-hydroxytryptophan (5-HTP), the immediate precursor
of 5-HT, into p-CP pretreated animals returns the serotonin
content of brain to normal and also returns the pain sensitivity
to normal (Tenen, 1967). More importantly, however, one can
also produce a reversal of the behavioral effects of a lesion.
Thus, injection of 5-HTP into rats with MFB lesions returns both
the brain serotonin content and pain sensitivity to normal values
in a dose dependent manner (Figure 2). This approach, allows
one to answer many of the questions raised in the Introduction to

----

TABLE 2

Effect of p-CP (300 mg/kg) and MFB Lesions
on Jump Thresholds and Brain Content of 5-HT

Experimental Group	Jump Threshold Milliamps	Serotonin Content (nanomoles/g) Telencephalon	Brain-Stem
Control	0.66 ± 0.04	3.75 ± 0.11	5.68 ± 0.37
Control + p-CP	$0.41 \pm 0.06^{*}$	$0.40 \pm 0.04^{*}$	$0.80 \pm 0.06^{*}$
MFB Lesion	$0.39 \pm 0.02^{*}$	$0.91 \pm 0.09^{*}$	5.34 ± 0.04
MFB Lesion + p-CP	$0.32 \pm 0.04^{*}$	$0.34 \pm 0.06^{*}$	$0.68 \pm 0.06^{*}$

All values are given as the mean $\pm$ S.E.M. Values are based on
4-16 animals.

*Indicates a mean value significantly different from controls
($p < 0.01$).

this paper. First of all, one can demonstrate the association
between the behavioral effects of a lesion and a known anatomical
system having a specific chemical composition. Secondly, one
can manipulate this chemical system in the lesioned animal to
verify that this is indeed the mechanism by which the lesion
produces its behavioral effects. Finally, one can manipulate
this system in the nonlesioned animal to produce predicted
effects on behavior. This approach has now been employed in
several situations to demonstrate that the behavioral effects
of a lesion are associated with the interruption of cholinergic
(Sorensen and Harvey, 1971), serotonergic (Jouvet, 1973), or
catecholaminergic (Ungerstedt, 1971b; Oltmans and Harvey, 1972)
pathways.

As might be expected from what has been said above, stimulation
of the monoaminergic cell bodies in brain stem results in an
increased turnover and release of putative synaptic transmitters
in telencephalon. For example, stimulation of the raphe nuclei
results in an increased turnover of 5-HT in telencephalon as
measured by: 1) decreases in brain 5-HT content and increases
in 5-hydroxyindoleacetic acid, the immediate metabolic product
of 5-HT (Sheard and Aghajanian, 1968a; Kostowski, et al., 1969);
2) increased conversion of ^{3}H-tryptophan to 5-HT (Shields and
Eccleston, 1972); and 3) increased release of 5-HT (Eccleston,
et al., 1969; Holman and Vogt, 1972). Such stimulation was also
found to block habituation of noise elicited startle. Depletion
of brain 5-HT by pretreatment of the animals with p-CP blocked
these behavioral effects of raphe stimulation (Sheard and
Aghajanian, 1968b). These results suggest that the effects of
brain stimulation can also be related to anatomical and chemical
systems in brain.

A number of drugs are now available to produce specific effects
on monoaminergic systems in the brain. The ability of p-CP to
deplete brain content of 5-HT through the inhibition of
tryptophan-5-hydroxylase (Koe and Weissman, 1966) has been
mentioned above. Similarly, α-methyl-p-tyrosine (AMPT) produces
an inhibition of tyrosine hydroxylase (Spector, et al., 1965)
with the consequent depletion of NE and DA content of brain.
The effects of both AMPT and p-CP are temporary so that one can
observe the animal's behavior during the depletion and repletion
of these transmitters. Drugs are also available that will produce specific and irreversible destruction of monoaminergic
neurons. Thus, depending on dosage one can produce a selective

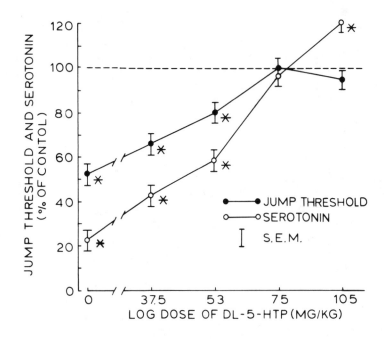

FIGURE 2

Effect of DL-5-HTP on jump threshold and telencephalic content
of serotonin in rats with medial forebrain bundle lesions.
DL-5-HTP was injected intraperitoneally 30 minutes prior to
testing of animals. At the termination of testing (80 minutes
after 5-HTP injection) animals were decapitated and brains
analyzed for serotonin content. For details see Harvey and
Lints. Each point represents the average of 4-5 animals.
Asterisks indicate a significant difference from control value
(p<0.05).

degeneration of the catecholamine neurons in brain by the intraventricular injection of 6-hydroxydopamine. Similarly, p-
chloroamphetamine produces a specific and irreversible damage to
the raphe cell bodies (Yunger, McMaster and Harvey, unpublished
data) and this results in the degeneration of the serotonergic
fiber system and a loss of serotonin in brain (Gál, et al., 1974).
Clearly, these drugs provide a valuable adjunct to the interpretation of lesion effects on behavior. However, there are
some anomalous effects of both lesions and drugs that should be
taken into account. For example, raphe lesions or p-CP do not
produce an inhibition of tryptophan-5-hydroxylase activity in
the septal area, though 5-HT content is reduced (Harvey and
Gál, 1974).

CENTRAL ADMINISTRATION OF DRUGS

It has now become a common practice to employ the central application of drugs or putative synaptic transmitters to examine
effects on behavior. Compounds are either administered intraventricularly or directly into brain tissue as crystals or
liquid injections. A number of problems arise with these
procedures. In the case of intraventricular injections, we
clearly do not know the site of drug action. Investigators
frequently assume that the compounds injected into brain tissue
are acting within the vicinity of the cannula tip, diffusing into
approximately 1 to 2 mm^3 of tissue (Grossman and Stumpf, 1969).
However, it has been demonstrated that the effects of angiotensin
injected into brain tissue are due to the diffusion of the
compound along the outer cannula and into the ventricles (Johnson,
et al., 1974). Thus, if the cannula is implanted so that it does
not pass through a ventricle no effect of the injected drug is
seen. Furthermore, much smaller dosages of the drug may be
required for intraventricular as compared to intra-tissue
injections. Diffusion may also depend on the amount of drug
administered, so that the effects of an intracerebral
injection can be due to the diffusion of a drug into the
systemic circulation with a consequent pharmacological effect
on peripheral tissue (Houpt and Epstein, 1971).

Another problem relates to the dosages of drug or putative
synaptic transmitter employed. Table 3 lists the highest
contents of four putative synaptic transmitters that have been
measured in specific brain regions: the caudate nucleus for
dopamine and acetylcholine and the diencephalon for serotonin
and norepinephrine. The average brain content is also given

for comparison purposes. Norepinephrine is typically injected intraventricularly or into tissue at a dosage of 10 μg or more, a dosage that is more than 13 times the entire amount of norepinephrine (0.76 μg) in the brain of a rat. If one assumes that the drug does not diffuse into more than 2 mm^3 of tissue then this would represent a content of 5 mg/g tissue or more than 2,000 times the highest reported endogenous content. It is difficult to understand why such large amounts would be required to produce an effect on behavior. It has been demonstrated that drinking can be reliably elicited by injection of 50 ng of angiotensin in the rat (Epstein, et al., 1970). This is a dosage of 50 pmoles. It has recently been shown that one can reduce the amount of NE required to affect eating if drug administration occurs at the time of initiation of feeding. Under these conditions, meal size is increased 180% by doses as low as 2.5 nanograms NE (Ritter, 1974). Again, assuming diffusion into 2 mm^3 of tissue this represents a local concentration of only 1.25 μg/g tissue, a value well within the endogenous content of NE in brain (Table 3). These results may alter our view of the role of NE in eating since these low dosages do not lead to an initiation of eating but do appear to determine meal size once eating has started. Both the data for angiotensin and NE quoted above, indicate that behavioral effects can be obtained with intracerebral dosages that are approximately 2-4 thousand times less than the dosages normally employed in such studies, suggesting that behavioral effects obtained with the higher dosages should be viewed with extreme caution. These findings also point to the need for adequate dose-response curves.

TABLE 3

Brain Contents of Putative Synaptic Transmitters

Compound and Molecular Weight	Average Brain Content μg/g	Highest Regional Content μg/g
Acetylcholine (146)	2.90	4.4
Dopamine (153)	0.60	9.0
Norepinephrine (169)	0.42	2.4
Serotonin (176)	0.63	2.3

There are powerful uptake mechanisms for all of the compounds listed in Table 3. It is possible therefore that a large proportion of the compounds being applied to the brain are being taken up by neuronal as well as glial elements so that their final concentration in the extracellular space is lower than the previous calculations would suggest. However, at the concentrations of compounds employed in most experiments, these uptake mechanisms would not be very specific. The application of even nanogram quantities of norepinephrine into the brain would be expected to produce a large inhibition (50% or more) of serotonin uptake, thus possibly affecting serotonergic neurons in the brain (Shaskan and Snyder, 1970). It is therefore necessary to know more about the precise distribution of the putative synaptic transmitters after they have been placed into the brain, both in terms of the extent of diffusion and in terms of their distribution in various cellular and subcellular compartments at the time that a behavioral effect is noted.

It is commonly assumed that an intracerebrally applied putative synaptic transmitter produces its effects by an action on some postsynaptic site. Blocking of the effects of a compound such as norepinephrine by an adrenergic blocking agent is put forth as further evidence for a postsynaptic locus of action. There is, however, no evidence to support such an interpretation, since we have no knowledge concerning the possible effects of these compounds on neural activity. When the electrophysiological response of cells is monitored during microelectrophoretic administration of various compounds, one finds that each of the putative synaptic transmitters listed in Table 3 can produce excitation of some cells and inhibition of others. The type of response depends on the area of the brain and type of cell being examined. It is thus not clear whether the intracerebral injection of the much larger quantities of putative synaptic transmitters produce their effects on behavior by neural excitation, inhibition, or both. Certainly, one would expect that such concentrations would produce desensitization of receptors as has been demonstrated for acetylcholine in CNS (Curtis and Ryall, 1966). Furthermore, the putative synaptic transmitters and their antagonists do not always produce effects on the electrophysiological response of central neurons that would be predicted from their pharmacologic classification (Curtis and Crawford, 1969; Bloom, et al., 1973). The effect of norepinephrine on cell firing in the brain stem or pyriform cortex is often not antagonized by either alpha- or beta-adrenergic blocking agents (Curtis and Crawford, 1969), and serotonin is often not blocked by its presumed antagonists (Bloom, et al., 1973). Atropine has effects on some central neurons that are not due to a specific muscarinic blockade, but rather are similar to the neuronal depression produced by procaine, a local anesthetic (Curtis and Phillis, 1960). In some cases blocking agents can have effects not seen in the peripheral nervous system. Both atropine and scopolamine have been shown to produce an increased release of acetylcholine from brain with a concomitant decrease in its brain content. This effect is noted whether the compounds are applied systemically or directly onto the cortex (Giarman and Pepeu, 1962, 1964; Mitchell, 1963; Szerb, 1964). The classification of agonists and antagonists has been established by experiments conducted on the peripheral autonomic nervous system or on the neuromuscular junction. It is becoming increasingly obvious that this classification system will not be identical for neurons of the central nervous system. Furthermore, as noted above, any given agent has multiple actions, and thus the precise action obtained in any given experiment will depend on dosage.

Even if one could demonstrate that these compounds are indeed producing their effects on some postsynaptic site, one cannot conclude that they are the normal synaptic transmitters. For example, GABA, a presumed synaptic transmitter, has been shown to have a potent electrophysiological effect on the cells of the nodose ganglion, and this effect can be blocked by bicuculline, an antagonist of GABA (DeGroat, 1972). Nevertheless, it is clear that GABA cannot be a synaptic transmitter in this ganglion since there is no endogenous GABA present. For this reason one must at least be able to demonstrate that the cells being exposed to an intracerebral injection of norepinephrine are indeed innervated by noradrenergic nerve terminals.

It is clear from what has been said that we do not yet understand the series of events occurring between the application of a compound into the brain and the elicitation or blocking of behavior. The intracerebral application of compounds, then, may provide us with some interesting data, but it cannot serve as the sole basis for inferring neurochemical functions without either the use of alternative methods or an analysis of the precise pharmacological and electrophysiological effects occurring when substances are applied in this manner to the brain.

PERIPHERAL ADMINISTRATION OF DRUGS

Much of what has been said above also applies to the peripheral
injection of drugs. A true pharmacological analysis of behavior
must involve the use of dose-effect curves and a calculation of
ED-50's, that is the dosage at which one obtains a 50% change
in some measure. Often experimenters employ one or two dosages
of a drug to determine effects on behavior. This can be misleading since almost every drug has biphasic effects, and so one
should cover the entire range of dosages. Furthermore, several
drugs should be examined to determine drug specificity and several
behaviors should be examined to determine behavioral specificity.
It is important that such studies be adequately descriptive since
we do not have definitive knowledge for the mechanism of action
of any centrally acting drug.

It is often thought that drugs might be classified by their
actions on specific categories of behavior. Thus, just as one
has convulsant and anti-convulsant drugs, analgesics, etc., one
might also find drugs that specifically affect aggression, anxiety, etc. However, there is little evidence as yet for such
specificity of drug action on categories of behavior (Harvey,
1971). Rather, the effects of a drug often depend on the precise
manner in which behavior is scheduled rather than on the
category of the behavior itself. For example, amphetamine
produces increases in an animal's rate of responding when the
reinforcer is either water, food, brain stimulation, or electric
shock. In each case the increase in rate of responding only
occurs under conditions that generate low base-line rates.
Similarly, tranquilizers and barbiturates can produce both
increases and decreases in the occurrence of a behavior that may
be independent of the reinforcer employed, but critically
dependent on the schedule of reinforcement. Indeed, it often
can be shown that the same dosage of drug can produce both
increases or decreases in responding in the same animal, the
direction of the effect depending simply on which of two
schedules of reinforcement are in effect (Harvey, 1971). Such
effects can also be seen in the peripheral actions of drugs.
Thus, the action of amphetamine on the small intestine is
dependent on the current activity of the muscle. During digestive
activity amphetamine may cause relaxation of the intestine, but
if the intestine is already relaxed, amphetamine may produce
contraction.

In spite of these cautionary notes, one can examine the mechanism by which drugs affect behavior. It is now generally agreed that most drugs exert their behavioral effects through an action on synaptic events, that is, by modifying the effects of particular synaptic transmitters. A great deal of information concerning the mechanism of drug action can therefore be obtained by examining the changes in drug action following lesions or drugs that produce a destruction of the monoaminergic or cholinergic pathways in brain. Thus, it has been shown that the behavioral effects of amphetamine are blocked by lesions or drugs that destroy the catecholaminergic but not by those destroying the serotonergic pathways in brain (Ungerstedt, 1971b; Green and Harvey, 1974). Similarly, AMPT which depletes catecholamines in brain also blocks amphetamine action (Weissman, et al., 1966; Dominic and Moore, 1969). These results suggest that amphetamine acts indirectly through the catecholaminergic systems, presumably by releasing catecholamines from nerve terminals.

CONCLUSION

Recent developments in neuropharmacology, neurochemistry and neuroanatomy provide the contemporary student of brain function with a variety of techniques and thus the ability to perform manipulations and measurements not previously possible. In addition, we now know that brain lesions, stimulation or drugs produce effects on behavior that are mediated via changes in the functional amounts of putative synaptic transmitters that are localized within defined anatomical systems. It is no longer desirable, therefore, to employ a single technique in the biological analysis of behavior. Rather, we have the possibility of a unitary view concerning the mechanism by which a variety of methods affect behavior and an ability to relate behavior to anatomy, neurochemistry, and physiology.

References

Aghajanian, G.K., Bloom, F.E., and Sheard, M.H. Brain Res., 1969, 13, 266.

Andén, N.E., Carlsson, A., Dahlström, A., Fuxe, K., Hillarp, N.Å., and Larsson, K. Life Sci., 1964, 3, 523.

Bloom, F.E., Hoffer, B.J., Nelson, C.N., Sheu, Y., and Siggins, G.R. In Serotonin and Behavior (J. Barchus and E. Usdin, Eds.). New York: Academic Press, 1973, p. 249.

Cannon, W.B. and Rosenblueth, A. The Supersensitivity of Denervated Structures: A Law of Denervation. New York: The MacMillan Co., 1937.

Curtis, D.R. and Crawford, J.M. Ann. Rev. Pharmacol., 1969, 9, 209.

Curtis, D.R. and Phillis, J.W. J. Physiol. (Lond), 1960, 153, 17.

Curtis, D.R. and Ryall, R.W. Exp. Brain Res., 1966, 2, 81.

Dahlström, A. and Fuxe, K. Acta Physiol. Scand. 62, 1964, Suppl. 232, 1.

De Groat, W.C. Brain Res., 1972, 38, 429.

Dominic, J.A. and Moore, K.E. Archs. Int. Pharmacodyn. Ther., 1969, 178, 166.

Eccleston, D., Ranic, M., Roberts, M.H.T., and Straughan, D.W. In Metabolism of Amines in Brain (G. Hooper, Ed.). London: MacMillan, 1969, p. 29.

Falck, B. and Hillarp, H.Å. Acta Anatomica, 1959, 38, 277.

Gál, E.M., Christiansen, P.A., and Yunger, L.M. Neuropharmacol., 1974, in press.

Giarman, N.J. and Pepeu, G. Brit. J. Pharmacol., 1962, 19, 226.

Giarman, N.J. and Pepeu, G. Brit. J. Pharmacol., 1964, 23, 123.

Green, T.K. and Harvey, J.A. J. Pharmacol. Exptl. Therap., 1974, in press.

Grossman, S.P. and Stumpf, W.E. Science, 1969, 166, 1410.

Harvey, J.A. Behavioral Analysis of Drug Action. Chicago:
    Scott-Foresman, 1971.

Harvey, J.A. and Lints, C.E. Science, 1965, 148, 250.

Harvey, J.A. and Lints, C.E. J. Comp. Physiol. Psychol., 1971,
    74, 28.

Harvey, J.A. and Gál, E.M. Science, 1974, 183, 869.

Harvey, J.A., Heller, A., and Moore, R.Y. J. Pharmacol. Exptl.
    Therap., 1963, 140, 103.

Harvey, J.A., Schlosberg, A.J., and Yunger, L.M. Fed. Proc.,
    1974, in press.

Harvey, J.A., Scholfield, C.N., Graham, L.T., and Aprison, M.H.
    Trans. Amer. Soc. Neurochem., 1974, 5.

Hedreen, J.C. and Chalmers, J.P. Brain Res., 1972, 47, 1.

Heller, A. and Harvey, J.A. The Pharmacol., 1963, 5, 264.

Heller, A., Harvey, J.A., and Moore, R.Y. Biochem. Pharmacol.,
    1962, 11, 859.

Hökfelt, T. Brain Res., 1970, 22, 147.

Holman, R.B. and Vogt, M. J. Physiol. (Lond), 1972, 223, 243.

Houpt, K.A. and Epstein, A.N. Physiol. Beh., 1971, 7, 897.

Jackson, J.H. (1898) In Selected Writings of John Hughlings
    Jackson, Vol. 2 (J. Taylor, Ed.). London: Staple
    Press, 1958, p. 422.

Johnson, A.K. In Control Mechanisms of Thirst (J.T. Fitzsimons,
    G. Peters, and L. Peters, Eds.). Heidelberg:
    Springer-Verlag, 1974.

Jouvet, M. In Serotonin and Behavior (J. Barchus and E. Usdin,
    Eds.). New York: Academic Press, 1973, p. 385.

Koe, B.K. and Weissman, A. J. Pharmacol. Exptl. Therap., 1966,
        154, 499.

Kostowski, W., Giacalone, E., Garattini, S., and Valzelli, L.
        Eur. J. Pharmacol., 1969, 7, 170.

Kuhar, M.J., Aghajanian, G.K., and Roth, R.H. Brain Res., 1972,
        44, 165.

Kuhar, M.J., Sethy, V.H., Roth, R.H., and Aghajanian, G.K. J.
        Neurochem., 1973, 20, 281.

Lewis, P.R. and Shute, C.C.D. Brain, 1967, 90, 521.

Manakow, Von C. (1911) In The Cerebral Cortex (G. Von Bonin,
        Ed.). Springfield: Charles C. Thomas, 1960, p. 231.

Margolis, F.L. Science, 1974, 184, 909.

Mitchell, J.P. J. Physiol. (Lond), 1963, 165, 98.

Octmans, G.A. and Harvey, J.A. Physiol. Beh., 1972, 8, 69.

Pepeu, G., Mulas, A., Ruffi, A., and Sotgiu, P. Life Sci., 1971,
        10, 181.

Ritter, R.C. Unpublished Ph.D. Dissertation, Univ. Pennsyl., 1974

Shaskan, E.G. and Snyder, S.H. J. Pharmacol. Exptl. Therap.,
        1970, 175, 404.

Sheard, M.H. and Aghajanian, G.K. J. Pharmacol. Exptl. Therap.,
        1968a, 163, 425.

Sheard, M.H. and Aghajanian, G.K. Life Sci., 1968b, 7, 19.

Shields, P.J. and Eccleston, D. J. Neurochem., 1972, 19, 265.

Shute, C.C.D. and Lewis, P.R. Brain, 1967, 40, 497.

Simpson, J.R., Grabarits, F., and Harvey, J.A. The Pharmacol.,
        1967, 9, 213.

Snyder, S.H., Young, A.B., Bennett, J.P., and Mulder, A.H. Fed.
        Proc., 1973, 32, 2039.

Sorensen, J.P., Jr. and Harvey, J.A. Physiol. Beh., 1971, 6, 723.

Spector, S., Sjoerdsma, A., and Udenfriend, S. J. Pharmacol. Exptl. Therap., 1965, 147, 86.

Szerb, J.C. Canad. J. Physiol. Pharmacol., 1964, 42, 303.

Tenen, S.S. Psychopharmacologia, 1967, 10, 204.

Ungerstedt, U. Acta Physiol. Scand., 1971a, Suppl. 367, 1.

Ungerstedt, U. Acta Physiol. Scand., 1971b, Suppl. 367, 69.

Weissman, A., Koe, B.K., and Tenen, S.S. J. Pharmacol. Exptl. Therap., 1966, 151, 339.

Zigmond, M.J., Chalmers, J.P., Simpson, J.R., and Wurtman, R.J, J. Pharmacol. Exptl. Therap., 1971, 179, 20.

Acknowledgment: Supported by USPHS Grant MH-16841-06.

HORMONE-BEHAVIOR ANALYSIS

Richard E. Whalen

University of California

Irvine, California 92664

Current research on hormones and behavior deals with two
distinct, but related aspects of hormone action, the effects
of hormones on behavior controlled by a fixed substrate and
the effects of hormones on the development and differentiation
of the substrate for behavior. These have often been called
the "activating" and "organizing" actions of hormones, respectively. Within the context of both of these modes of action
of hormones, I would like to discuss certain methodological
considerations and contemporary approaches to the endocrinological analysis of behavior.

Behavioral Activation

The classical approach of the endocrinologist to the question
of the function of a gland first involves the extirpation of
the gland followed by the measurement of some physiological
parameter. The same approach is followed by the behavioral
endocrinologist. With respect to aggressive behavior it is
well known that castration is followed by a reduction in
aggressivity in a wide variety of species (Guhl, 1961), although this effect is not always found (Karli, 1958). In
such studies it is important to test the animals at varying

times after castration since a change in behavior may not become
evident for some weeks following gonadectomy (Davidson, 1966).

The second step in the endocrine analysis is to restore preoperative function by the application of exogenous hormones.
During the past 25 years students of sexual and aggressive
behavior have accomplished this by administering synthetic
esterified hormones such as testosterone propionate (TP) or
estradiol benzoate (EB). The esterified hormones were used
because they were readily available as generous gifts of
pharmaceutical houses and because they are usually more potent
than the free forms of the steroids. This approach is illustrated by Edwards' (1969) data. In this study male and female

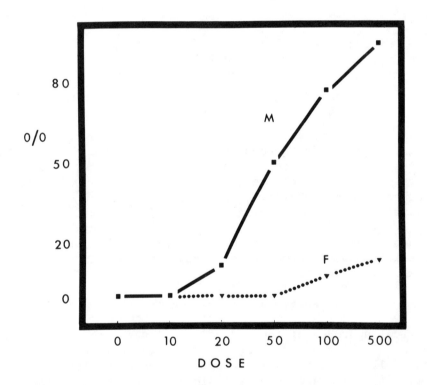

Figure 1. Effects of oil or varying doses of testosterone
propionate during adulthood on the percentage of male and
female mice fighting. Data from Edwards, 1969.

Swiss-Webster mice were gonadectomized at 30 days of age; testing began at 60 days of age. Prior to the first test the animals were injected with oil and prior to subsequent tests they were injected with TP. Figure 1 reveals several interesting points. First, the gonadectomized male mice failed to fight when given control injections. Most intact males would have fought under these conditions. Second, fighting behavior can be restored in males by TP. Third, the degree of restoration is a function of the hormone dose. This is an important point often ignored by investigators. A careful dose-response analysis is a critical component of any study of hormone-behavior relationships. And, fourth, males and females respond differently to hormone treatment. Unlike males, females rarely fight under these conditions, even when administered large doses of male hormone.

Active Agent. Studies such as that of Edwards are very useful in that they indicate that the behavior in question is indeed under hormonal control and because they define quantitatively some of the critical parameters involved. Such studies do not, however, answer the question of what is the active agent. The assumption that the active agent is testosterone is not justified. Since the important papers of Anderson and Liao and Bruchovsky and Wilson in 1968, we have known that the nuclei of the prostate, an androgen-dependent tissue, concentrate predominately the 5 α -reduced metabolite of testosterone, dihydrotestosterone. It is therefore possible that behavioral changes observed after TP treatment are not due to testosterone, but to one of its androgenic metabolites. Luttge (1972; Luttge and Hall, 1973) has examined this possibility by treating castrated CD-1 and Swiss-Webster male mice with either testosterone or dihydrotestosterone. The findings are shown in Figure 2. With both strains, testosterone was found to be more effective than dihydrotestosterone in inducing fighting behavior, suggesting that testosterone may be the active agent.

The Luttge studies also showed that the CD-1 males were more responsive to testosterone than were the S-W males; the opposite was true for response to dihydrotestosterone. Thus, one must remain aware of the role of genome in hormone-behavior studies. This point was dramatically illustrated to us recently in our work (Gorzalka and Whalen, 1974) on the action of progestins on mouse sexual behavior. Ovariectomized female mice of the CD-1 and S-W strains were administered estrogen and progesterone

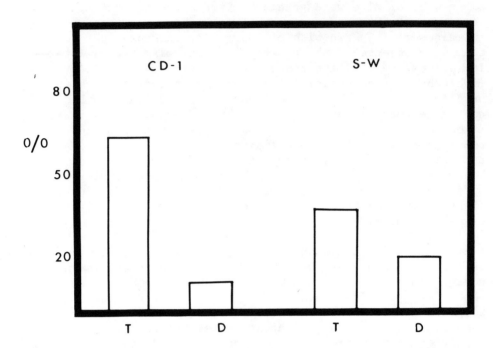

Figure 2. Percentage of castrated male CD-1 and Swiss-Webster
mice fighting following treatment with either testosterone (T)
or dihydrotestosterone (D). Data from Luttge, 1972; Luttge
and Hall, 1973.

each week and were tested for sexual receptivity. The intensity of receptivity progressively increased. On Week 7 the
animals were given estrogen and dihydroprogesterone (DHP).
Neither strain responded. After several weeks of treatment
and testing the CD-1 females responded fully to DHP as they
had earlier to progesterone. The S-W females never responded
to DHP. Thus, one strain was responsive to both progesterone
and to its reduced metabolite, while the other strain responded
only to progesterone.

Returning to the question of hormone metabolism, most of the
studies done to date have failed to show that any androgenic

metabolite of testosterone is more potent than the parent compound with respect to behavior. Payne (1973), however, has stated that androstenedione, which is both a metabolite of testosterone and a secretory product of the testis, is more potent than dihydrotestosterone or testosterone propionate in inducing aggression in castrated male hamsters. This study suffers, however, in that only one dose of each hormone was used and because free forms, e.g. androstenedione, were compared with esterified forms, e.g. TP. Such comparisons are of little value because of the different dose-response characteristics of free and esterified hormones.

A second aspect of the question of the active agent also concerns hormone metabolism, aromatization, in particular. It has been demonstrated that androgens can be aromatized to estrogens by brain tissue, testosterone to estradiol and androstenedione to estrone, as examples. Naftolin and his colleagues (Naftolin, Ryan and Petro, 1972; Reddy, Naftolin and Ryan, 1973) have recently argued that this metabolic step is important in the mechanism of action of the androgens. Thus, it might be suggested that testosterone mediates aggressive behavior only after being converted to estrogen. Support for this notion has come from studies which have shown that non-aromatizing androgens such as DHT and androsterone fail to maintain or restore mating in castrated male rats (Feder, 1971; Whalen and Luttge, 1971; Beyer, Larsson, Perez-Palacios and Morali, 1973). Although a great deal of attention has been paid to this hypothesis recently, it is now clear that it is of limited generality. Dihydrotestosterone, which is non-aromatizing, while relatively ineffective in the rat, can maintain mating behavior in rabbits (Beyer and Rivaud, 1973), and in CD-1 male mice (Luttge and Hall, 1973). In our laboratory J. DeBold and I have found that DHT will maintain mating in male hamsters.

In spite of the fact that the evidence favors the hypothesis that the normally secreted androgens are behaviorally active, one cannot dismiss the potential role of hormone metabolism in hormone action. Treatment of animals with testosterone or dihydrotestosterone leads to the accumulation of a variety of metabolites in the brain (Whalen and Rezek, 1972) which could in fact interact in the control of behavior. Attention is directed to this possibility by recent studies which have shown that it is possible to induce mating in male rats with a combination of estrogen and dihydrotestosterone in doses

which are ineffective when used alone (Baum and Vreeburg, 1973).
This suggests the possibility, which must be explored, that
testosterone acts by a combination of aromatization and 5 α -
reduction processes.

Locus of Action. Given that we can ultimately determine the
nature of the active agent, our next question would concern the
location of action of the hormone or metabolite. Most studies
done to date have used the systemic administration of hormones,
a technique which does not allow for localization. Several
years ago Harris, Michael and Scott (1958) demonstrated that
one could induce sexual receptivity in female cats by implanting
into the diencephalon needles with small amounts of estrogen
fused to the tip. These implants were effective only in
certain loci; moreover, these implants did not produce peripheral estrogenic effects. Similar effects have been demonstrated
by Davidson (1966) and Johnston and Davidson (1972) using
androgens and examining male mating behavior.

Implantation studies are rather easy to carry out when one is
studying the actions of estrogens. These steroids are extremely potent and as a result one is able to use small implants
and obtain reasonably precise localization. The problem becomes more difficult when working with androgens. With these
steroids the implants must be rather large (Johnston and
Davidson used 20 ga cannulae). The large cannulae can produce
a great deal of brain damage and they increase the possibility
that the steroid will spread into the systemic circulation.
Kierniesky and Gerall (1973) recently ran into this latter
problem. These workers implanted 20 ga cannulae containing
TP into rat brain. They were not able to selectively activate
mating behavior because the implants allowed sufficient
androgen into the systemic circulation to maintain some
peripheral target tissues. With respect to aggressive behavior, Owen, Peters and Bronson (1974) ran into the same
problem when they implanted TP into mouse brain using 26 ga
needles. Only when they reduced the cannulae size and the
concentration of the hormone were they able to show that
fighting could be selectively elicited by implants in the
septum and preoptic area but not by implants into the amygdala
or reticular formation.

Finally, with respect to localization, implantation procedures
must be given careful consideration. A number of studies

which have demonstrated the induction of behavior change with
local implants of hormone have found medial preoptic-anterior
hypothalamic sites to be active. In the normal course of
approaching these sites the implanted cannulae pierce the
ventricle. The possibility therefore exists that the hormone
is effective by leaking up the shaft of the cannula and into
the ventricle. It appears that this is the mechanism by which
implants of angiotensin into the preoptic region activate
drinking. To avoid this problem implants can be placed in the
same region via different routes. We faced this problem
recently in a study of the inhibitory effects of Actinomycin-D
on estrogen-induced mating in female rats (Whalen, Quadagno,
DeBold and Gorzalka, unpubl.). Quadagno, Shryne and Gorski
(1971) had shown that if estrogen treatment is followed 12 hrs.
later by implants of Actinomycin-D into the preoptic area the
estrogen failed to induce heat. We asked whether this was due
to a local effect of the antibiotic in the preoptic region or
to a ventricular effect. We found that Actinomycin-D implants
into the caudate were ineffective, even if the cannulae
pierced the ventricles and that such implants were effective
in inhibiting estrogen action in the preoptic region even if
the cannulae did not pierce the ventricles.

I feel that these studies show that it is possible to study
the location of hormone action in the brain, but they also
show that care must be taken to insure that the observed
effects are not due to a spread of the hormone or chemical
into the systemic circulation or into the ventricular system.

Non-specific Effects. Even though one can reliably induce a
hormone dependent response pattern by the systemic application
of a hormone or chemical, one must still be concerned about
the specificity of that effect. Let us examine two examples.
Sodersten (1973) recently reported that he was able to induce
the full copulatory pattern in castrated male rats by the
administration of estradiol benzoate. This finding was
striking since one expects masculine behavior to be activated
by androgens and not by estrogen. We felt that this might be
a non-specific effect mediated by the adrenal system. The
adrenal is known to secrete androgens, particularly
androstenedione, and it is known that androstenedione is
capable of inducing copulatory behavior in rats (Whalen and
Luttge, 1971). Therefore, B. Gorzalka, D. Rezek and I
administered testosterone propionate or estradiol benzoate to
castrated, adrenally-intact male rats. As reported by

Sodersten, both treatments induced full ejaculatory behavior.
EB administered to castrated, adrenalectomized rats, however,
failed to induce ejaculatory behavior. When these
adrenalectomized males were subsequently administered TP
ejaculation was restored. Adrenalectomy of TP-treated males
did not influence ejaculatory behavior. Thus, the ejaculatory
behavior induced by estrogen is, in fact, mediated by some
action of the adrenal gland.

We have also found another presumed hormone effect which seems
to be mediated in a non-specific manner by the adrenal gland.
Clemens, Wallen and Gorski (1967) reported that it was possible
to mimic the effect of progesterone on receptivity in estrogen-
treated female rats by applying potassium chloride to the
cerebral cortex of estrogen-treated animals. They postulated
that the KCl permitted mating by a release of tonic cortical
inhibition and that progesterone might normally work in this
manner. We speculated that this effect may be non-specific
and mediated by the adrenal gland because of the possibility
that the cortical application of KCl might act as a generalized
stressor. Resko (1969) has shown that the adrenal is capable
of secreting substantial amounts of progesterone following
ACTH treatment and stress should do the same. Therefore,
B. Neubauer, B. Gorzalka and I applied KCl to the cortex of
estrogenized adrenally-intact and adrenalectomized female
rats. The KCl induced mating in the former, but not in the
latter group. When the adrenalectomized rats were subsequently
administered estrogen and progesterone they did show intense
receptive behavior. Thus, it is likely that the KCl acted not
directly on some cortical inhibitory process, but rather by
causing the release of ACTH and then adrenal progesterone.
These two examples are presented simply to demonstrate the
care one must take to avoid the possibility that a given
treatment is working not directly, but by some secondary
non-specific process.

Individual Differences. Finally, I would urge that attention
be paid to individual differences in hormone response. It is
well known to workers in the field that a given dose of
hormone may have a large behavioral effect in one animal while
having rather little effect in another (Whalen, 1974). However,
it should be noted that individual differences in hormone
response appear to reflect substrate sensitivity rather than
differences in circulating levels of hormones (Grunt and Young,
1952, 1953; Beach and Fowler, 1959).

Behavioral Differentiation

Since the work of Phoenix, Goy, Gerall and Young (1959) which showed that the female offspring of pregnant guinea pigs administered testosterone propionate were more likely to show masculine responses and less likely to show feminine responses than controls, numerous studies have been done on rats, mice, guinea pigs, hamsters, dogs, monkeys and even fowl demonstrating that hormone stimulation during sensitive periods of development can permanently alter behavioral responsiveness to hormones. These studies have been reviewed several times recently (Beach, 1971; Goy and Goldfoot, in press). While most of the work which has been done has focussed on sexual behavior, some of

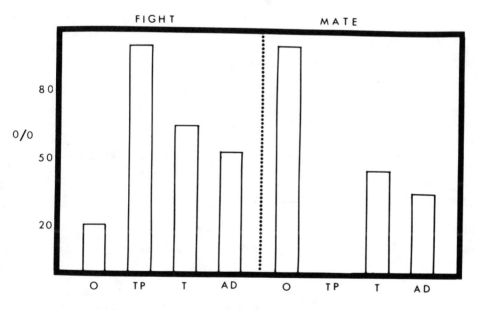

Figure 3. Percentage of female mice showing fighting behavior and mating behavior in adulthood following treatment with oil, testosterone propionate, testosterone or androstenedione in infancy. Data from Edwards, 1971.

the more recent work has examined the sexual differentiation
of aggressive behavior. Edwards (1969), for example, showed
that a single early postnatal injection of TP would facilitate
the display of isolation-induced fighting in female mice. More
recently Edwards (1971) compared the effects of postnatal
administration of oil, testosterone propionate, testosterone,
and androstenedione on the later display of fighting and mating
in female mice. Figure 3 shows the results of this experiment.
TP treatment greatly enhanced the probability of fighting and
eliminated the display of mating responses in these female
mice. Free testosterone had a lesser effect on both systems,
while free androstenedione was the least effective steroid in
modifying hormone sensitivity. This figure illustrates the
differential effectiveness of free and esterified testosterone
as well as the differential effectiveness of the naturally
secreted steroids.

Thus, the same questions exist when we consider the role of
hormones in the differentiation of behavioral control systems
as exist when we consider the role of hormones in the activation of behavior, namely, what hormones are active, what
are their dose-response relationships, what is the site of
action of these hormones, are the actions specific and what
is the nature of the individual differences in hormone action.
The only difference which exists between the study of differentiation and activation concerns the time of hormone action.
The studies done to date are convincing in showing that
organisms develop through periods during which they are
particularly sensitive to the action of hormones. Therefore,
an examination of the differentiation process should include
time-response studies, as well as the previously mentioned
components of any thorough hormone-behavior analysis.

References

Anderson, K.M. and Liao, S.   Selective retention of dihydro-
    testosterone by prostatic nuclei. Nature, 1968, 219,
    277-279.

Baum, M.J. and Vreeburg, J.T.M.   Copulation in castrated male
    rats following combined treatment with estradiol and
    dihydrotestosterone. Science, 1973, 182, 283-285.

Beach, F.A.   Hormonal factors controlling the differentiation
     development and display of copulatory behavior in the
     ramstergig and related species.   In The Biopsychology of
     Development (E. Tobach, L.R. Aronson and E. Shaw, Eds.)
     Academic Press, New York, 1971, 249-296.

Beach, F.A. and Fowler, H.   Individual differences in the
     response of male rats to androgen,   J. comp. physiol.
     Psychol., 1959, 52, 50-52.

Beyer, C., Larsson, K., Perez-Palacios, G. and Morali, G.
     Androgen structure and male sexual behavior in the
     castrated rat.   Horm. Behav., 1973, 4, 99-107.

Beyer, C. and Rivaud, N.   Differential effect of testosterone
     and dihydrotestosterone on the sexual behavior of
     prepuberally castrated male rabbits.   Horm. Behav., 1973,
     4, 175-180.

Bruchovsky, N. and Wilson, J.D.   The conversion of testosterone
     to 5 α -androstan-17 β -ol-3-one by rat prostate.   J. Biol.,
     Chem., 1968, 243, 5953-5960.

Clemens, L.G., Wallen, K. and Gorski, R.A.   Mating behavior:
     Facilitation in the female rat after cortical application
     of potassium chloride.   Science, 1967, 157, 1208-1209.

Davidson, J.M.   Characteristics of sex behaviour in male rats
     following castration.   Anim. Behav., 1966, 14, 266-272.

Davidson, J.M.   Activation of the male rat's sexual behavior
     by intracerebral implantation of androgen.   Endocrinology,
     1966, 79, 783-794.

Edwards, D.A.   Early androgen stimulation and aggressive
     behavior in male and female mice.   Physiol. Behav., 1969,
     4, 333-338.

Edwards, D.A.   Neonatal administration of androstenedione,
     testosterone or testosterone propionate: Effects on
     ovulation, sexual receptivity and aggressive behavior in
     female mice.   Physiol. Behav., 1971, 6, 223-228.

Feder, H.H.   The comparative actions of testosterone propionate
    and 5 α-androstan-17β-ol-3-one propionate on the
    reproductive physiology and morphology of male rats. J.
    Endocr., 1971, 51, 241-252.

Gorzalka, B.B. and Whalen, R.E.   Genetic regulation of hormone
    action: Selective effects of progesterone and dihydro-
    progesterone (5 α-pregnane-3,20-dione) on sexual recep-
    tivity in mice. Steroids, 1974, in press.

Goy, R.W. and Goldfoot, D.A.   Hormonal influence on sexually
    dimorphic behavior. In Handbook of Physiology:
    Endocrinology II. (R.O. Greep and E.B. Astwood, Eds.).
    Am. Physiol. Soc., Washington, D.C., in press.

Grunt, J.A. and Young, W.C.   Differential reactivity of
    individuals and the response of the male guinea pig to
    testosterone propionate. Endocrinology, 1952, 51, 237-
    248.

Grunt, J.A. and Young, W.C.   Consistency of sexual behavior
    patterns in individual male guinea pigs following
    castration and androgen therapy. J. comp. physiol.
    Psychol., 1953, 46, 138-144.

Guhl, A.M.   Gonadal hormones and social behavior in infrahuman
    vertebrates. In Sex and Internal Secretions, (W.C. Young,
    Ed.) Williams and Wilkins Co., Baltimore, 1961, vol. 2
    Pp 1240-1267.

Harris, G.W., Michael, R.P. and Scott, P.O.   Neurological
    site of action of stilboestrol in eliciting sexual
    behaviour. In Neurological Basis of Behavior. (G.E.W.
    Wolstenholme and C.M. O'Connor, Eds.) Little, Brown and
    Co., Boston, 1958, Pp. 236-251.

Johnston, P. and Davidson, J.M.   Intracerebral androgens and
    sexual behavior in the male rat. Horm. Behav., 1972,
    3, 345-357.

Karli, P.   Hormones steroides et comportement d'agression
    interspecifique Rat-Souris. J. de Physiol., (Paris),
    1958, 50, 346-347.

Kierniesky, N.C. and Gerall, A.A.   Effects of testosterone
    propionate implants in the brain on the sexual behavior
    and peripheral tissues of the male rat. Physiol. Behav.,
    1973, 11, 633-640.

Luttge, W.G.   Activation and inhibition of isolation induced
    inter-male fighting behavior in castrate male CD-1 mice
    treated with steroidal hormones. Horm. Behav., 1972, 3,
    71-81.

Luttge, W.G. and Hall, N.R.   Androgen-induced agonistic
    behavior in castrate male Swiss-Webster mice: Comparison
    of four naturally occurring androgens. Behav. Biol.,
    1973, 8, 725-732.

Naftolin, F., Ryan, K.J. and Petro, Z.   Aromatization of
    androstenedione by the anterior hypothalamus of adult male
    and female rats. Endocrinology, 1972, 90, 295-298.

Owen, K., Peters, P.J. and Bronson, F.H.   Effects of intra-
    cerebral implants of testosterone propionate in intermale
    aggression in the castrated male mouse. Horm. Behav.,
    1974, 5, 83-92.

Payne, A.P.   The effect of androgens on isolation-induced
    aggression in the male golden hamster. J. Endocr., 1973,
    57, xxxvi.

Phoenix, C.H., Goy, R.W., Gerall, A.A. and Young, W.C.
    Organizing action of prenatally administered testosterone
    propionate on the tissues mediating mating behavior in
    the female guinea pig. Endocrinology, 1959, 65, 369-382.

Quadagno, D.M., Shryne, J. and Gorski, R.A.   The inhibition
    of steroid-induced sexual behavior by intrahypothalamic
    Actinomycin-D. Horm. Behav., 1971, 2, 1-10.

Reddy, V.V.R., Naftolin, F. and Ryan, K.J.   Aromatization in
    the central nervous system of rabbits: Effects of
    castration and hormone treatment. Endocrinology, 1973,
    92, 589-594.

Resko, J.A.   Endocrine control of adrenal progesterone
    secretion in the ovariectomized rat. Science, 1969,
    164, 70-71.

Sodersten, P.   Estrogen-activated sexual behavior in male rats.
     Horm. Behav., 1973, 4, 247-256.

Whalen, R.E.   Estrogen-progesterone induction of mating in
     female rats. Horm. Behav., 1974, in press.

Whalen, R.E. and Luttge, W.G.   Testosterone, androstenedione
     and dihydrotestosterone: Effects on mating behavior of
     male rats. Horm. Behav., 1971, 2, 117-125.

Whalen, R.E. and Rezek, D.L.   Localization of androgenic
     metabolites in the brain of rats administered testosterone
     or dihydrotestosterone. Steroids, 1972, 20, 717-725.

DISCUSSION

Leshner: There are a few lines of evidence which suggest that the adrenals are important for aggressive behavior and that their effects are independent of effects on androgen secretion.

Whalen: That is a good point to remember. There certainly are studies which implicate adrenal function in aggression. I only meant to suggest that the adrenals seem to play little role in normal reproductive function.

Barkley: In some of our recent work we have found a differential sensitivity to testosterone of behavior and peripheral targets, the aggressive behavior being more sensitive to the hormone. The aggressive behavior declines following castration, but can be maintained with a very low dose of testosterone.

Whalen: One of the earliest demonstrations of that phenomenon was by Michael looking at the induction of receptivity in female cats. He found if you gave a low dose of estrogen you could induce the behavior before producing peripheral effects. With a high dose of hormone peripheral effects occurred before behavioral changes. Thus, it is clear that the central and peripheral tissues do have differential thresholds for response to hormones.

Harvey: Is there any kind of theory that is current about how the hormones are working. For example, are the effects being mediated by synaptic transmitters?

Whalen: There is no good theory about the action of the hormones in the brain. It is clear that the hormone can be bound in neural nuclei. We have obtained a little evidence that there may be protein synthesis that is induced by estrogen. Whether this is involved in the mechanism of

163

action of the hormone is still unclear, however.
It is possible that the effects are mediated by
changes in transmitters. For example, there
are changes in transmitter levels over the
estrous cycle, but I feel no one has tied them
closely to behavioral changes yet.

Plotnick: Have you studied hormones and sex or aggression
in monkeys?

Whalen: Richard Green and I studied dominance hierarchies in squirrel monkeys. We allowed
dominance relationships to become established
and then castrated the alpha male. We then
administered testosterone to the alpha female.
This was in colonies of three males and three
females. These manipulations had almost no
effect on either feeding or display behaviors.
We concluded that in this species the hormones
are probably not involved in the maintainance
of the dominance behavior. They could, however,
be involved in the establishment of hierarchies.

THE STUDY OF HUMAN AGGRESSION

John R. Lion and Manoel Penna

University of Maryland

Baltimore, Maryland 21201

Since the time of Pavlov, scientists have attempted to replicate emotional illness in man with animal models. In the
area of aggression, most researchers are familiar with experimental paradigms of isolation, footshock, and septal-lesion
induced aggression in rats and muricidal rats. Animal models
utilizing fighting fish or certain brain preparations of
other animals have been described as means of studying aggression. All these analogs of aggression have provided valuable data in the field of pharmacology and neurophysiology.
Parallels have been drawn between septal-induced aggression
in animals and humans with certain forms of brain dysfunction.
Here, the neurophysiology may be similar, but it is now well
known that there are distinct and remarkable behavioral differences between such species as cats, dogs, rats, and men
with regard to the psychological effects obtained from
lesions and stimulations of the same cortical areas. Analogies have been drawn between footshock or isolation-induced
aggression in rats and hyperirritable states in humans
ranging from hyperkinetic syndromes to the hypervigilant
states accompanying paranoid or paranoid psychotic states.
It is apparent, of course, but still necessary to point out

that there are vast phenomenological gaps in the assumption
of such analogies, and I submit to you that the relevance of
such models for studying human aggression may be questionable.
For example, muricidal rats are not like homicidal individuals,
for statistics demonstrate that homicidal individuals kill
one time and are not prone to repeated murders; further,
homicide is a distinct social act with a victim, an available
gun, alcohol, and social setting. No one animal can duplicate
these complex conditions. While there may indeed be humans
who kill for a living, such as members of organized crime, such
individuals are rare among the group of individuals committing
murder and, further, have never come to formal psychiatric
attention (Bromberg, 1965).

Equally questionable may be the human experiments on aggression such as the well known studies by Feshbach (1961),
Bandura (1963), or Milgram (1963). These experiments
cleverly demonstrate some of the social parameters of
aggression such as the effects of media violence or con-
formity and peer pressure, but they lack close resemblance
to the forms of violence which the clinician is apt to see
in prison or in a hospital or clinic setting. The striking
of bobo dolls is far removed from the assaulting of a
spouse by an alcoholic husband; even the more realistic
experiments where univeristy students give (fake) electric
shocks in a learning situation, while involving the inflict-
ing of "harm" on other humans, is more of a test of con-
formity than a simulation of sadism, vindictiveness, rage,
or murderous anger. Thus these types of studies, too, have
their limits in serving as analogues for human behavior.

In order to demonstrate more clearly the limitations of
laboratory studies of aggression, I should like to define
and describe the forms of human aggression which the clinician sees. First, let me at the outset say that aggression
is a symptom of an underlying psychological state. There
is no such thing as one aggressive patient, and in this
regard aggression is not like depression. This point is
often not fully realized. Most of us have a clear idea of
what a depressed patient is--he sits quietly in a corner
and displays psychomotor retardation, despondency, impov-
erishment of ideas, sad facies; he eats little, has insomnia
of some form, and cries. There are variants of depression

to be sure--there are agitated depressions and psychotic
depression, but there is generally cross cultural agreement
on what a depressed patient is and how he acts. This is not
the case at all with an aggressive patient, for the aggression may spring from a psychosis, or may be part of the picture
of a manic-depressive illness. It may be a result of a toxic
psychosis, such as that from amphetamines, or it may be part
of the picture of a paranoid schizophrenic illness, or it may
be part of an explosive or antisocial or passive-aggressive
personality structure, or, as we just discussed, it may even
stem from a psychotic depressive disorder. So when we say the
patient is aggressive we have to qualify what the basis of his
aggression is and make a diagnosis (Lion, 1972).

This is not the only problem, however, in dealing with
aggressive humans. There is also a problem of defining the
aggression. Murder, rape, armed robbery, and assault are
the FBI designated crimes of violence. But there are other
behavioral acts which are violent. A patient may hit his
wife and want treatment for what he perceives to be extreme
violence. In some subcultures, violence is more or less a
way of life and much higher thresholds are tolerated before
a patient identifies himself as violent. Thus not only do
we have a problem in diagnosing the etiology of violence,
but we also have to decide whether or not the act is pathological, and herein lies a sticky problem. And that problem
is this: Aggression is a useful human trait, if appropriately handled. We all need to be properly aggressive and
society needs aggressive individuals to carry out programs
of social reform. Therefore, aggression can be normal, and
it can be abnormal, and decisions as to which is which are
often subjective, involve our own moral and ethical and
psychological sets, and shape our opinions and our treatment
strategies and vigor. There is a continuum between healthy
and abnormal aggression, and the aim of the clinician who
treats a violent patient is not to suppress violence but to
get the patient to effectively modulate it himself to best
advantage. A drug which abolishes all assertiveness and
aggressiveness is no good, nor is a surgical procedure which
renders a patient totally placid. Aggressiveness must be
preserved for aggressiveness has adaptive human value.

To summarize: I have stated that aggression in humans is a
symptom of an underlying psychological condition, but I am
also saying that aggression can be healthy and normal.
Bearing this in mind, I now describe the varieties of what
I would consider deviant human aggression.

I think the most common form of deviant human aggression
occurs in the class of personality disorders labelled
variously as Explosive, Passive-aggressive, or Antisocial
(Lion, 1974a, in press). The bulk of prisoners in the jails
around our country are made up of individuals with this
diagnosis. Such patients demonstrate recurring and labile
hostile episodes, rage attacks, temper outbursts; some have
serious problems with impulse control and others, though
able to plan and premeditate criminal activity, are bothered
by paroxysmal aggressive and impulsive acts which severely
hamper their actions and lives. The way these prisoners
talk of themselves is to say that they have "short fuses",
"blow up easily", or just get "mean streaks." Whether or
not the "ictal-like" nature of their paroxysmal behavior
outbursts is reflective of brain dysfunction is a matter of
scientific interest to me and others who have done work in
this area; certain patients do demonstrate evidence of
epileptic disturbances while others merely show equivocal
neurological and EEG abnormalities and some evidence of
organicity on psychological testing (Bach-y-Rita et al, 1971;
Monroe, 1970; Lion et al, 1974).

Impulsivity, by the way, is an important conceptual part of
aggression in humans. Unlike a depressed patient who can
stay depressed most of the day during the period of his
depression, aggressive patients rarely remain aggressive for
sustained periods but, instead, show periods of aggressive
behavior which may or may not be superimposed upon a background of hostility or a psychosis with some degree of
agitation. Why this should be so is not clear; the best
explanation I can offer is that aggression is physiologically
so mobilizing that it would lead to somatic exhaustion if
it existed more than a few minutes or hours. Indeed, in
some cases of mania or catatonic excitement with agitation
and belligerence, physical exhaustion is a distinct medical
threat and therapeutic efforts often take on emergency
qualities in an attempt to sedate and quiet the patient to
prevent such exhaustion, much as one might sedate a patient

in status epilepticus who runs the risk of eventual brain
anoxia and permanent physical harm. Therefore, it is
important to realize and consider, when doing research on
aggression--in man, at least--the role of impulsivity and the
phenomenon of impulsivity in the expression of aggression in
man.

I have mentioned catatonic and manic related forms of
aggression, and so now describe a second diagnosis of
aggressive patients, the patient whose aggressiveness stems
from a thought disorder such as a schizophrenic illness, a
manic-depressive psychosis, or an involutional process. The
aggressiveness of such patients results from their disordered
thinking and lacks the peculiar and particular impulsivity
present in the former group of personality disordered
patients. Patients such as those with catatonic excitement
or paranoid schizophrenia often demonstrate combativeness,
belligerence, agitation, and other forms of aggression due
to delusional beliefs, auditory hallucinations, and paranoid
ideation. This class of aggressive patients is much
different from the personality disordered group--the
patients' aggressiveness stems from not poor impulse control,
but from disordered and abberant thinking. Incidentally,
patients with disordered thinking have been known to turn
their aggression inward and commit suicide as well as homicide, and the phenomenon of the introjection of aggression
is not uncommon in violent people of a more borderline
nature--i.e., those with impaired ego function who often
are close to psychosis. In our combined series of about
280 violent patients (Bach-y-Rita et al, 1971; Lion et al,
1974) 30% made serious suicide attempts, reflecting their
poor ability to cope with aggressive urges when the object
of their aggression was not available. This psychodynamic,
the externalization and internalization of aggression is
a subject that requires study and research in the future.

An interesting, though controversial third group of aggressive patients are those who demonstrate the so-called hyperkinetic behavior syndromes. These are usually children who
show low frustration tolerances to stress, impulsivity,
psychomotor agitation, and aggressiveness and belligerence.
Some of these children's hyperkinesis results from minimal
brain dysfunction and others show hyperkinetic behavior
secondary to psychogenic etiologies. More recent clinical
studies have shown adolescents to demonstrate states of

minimal brain dysfunction as evidenced by neurological,
psychological, and EEG findings (Harticollos, 1968) and
there is at least one anecdotal report (Arnold, 1972) in
the literature and one unpublished study (Lion and Monroe,
in press, 1974b) of this syndrome in adults who, like
children, benefitted from CNS stimulants. I shall return
to the treatment aspect of hyperkinesis later. In some
respects, the hyperkinetic aggressive youngster resembles
the explosive personality I described in the first category
of aggressive patients and I and co-workers have been
impressed with this similarity from the neuropyschiatric
point of view.

A fourth group of patients who demonstrate aggressiveness
are those with hypersexual disorders with concomitant
aggressive behavior, such as rapists or individuals
involved in repetitive sexual crimes involving force (Sturup,
1968). In some such instances, hypersexuality plays a
prominent role in the behavior so that we are talking about
a group of aggressive patients whose violence stems from a
qualitatively or quantitatively deviant sexual drive. These
patients are driven to aggressive acts on the basis of a
recurring need to fulfill a particular sexual perversion;
the perversion usually entails orgasm and a reduction in
sexual tension, so that this type of patient requires treatment efforts considerably different from other types of
violent patients.

Another group of patients demonstrate violence as a result
of a toxic state. I refer here to toxic paranoid psychoses
induced by alcohol, amphetamine usage, LSD ingestion, or
other CNS stimulants or hallucinogens (Ellenwood, 1971;
Bach-y-Rita et al, 1970). Any alteration in brain function
can lead to violence and we are all familiar with the DT
patient who becomes combative as he goes through alcohol
detoxification. A ubiquitous class of intermittently
combative patients are those with organic brain syndromes
who become confused, disoriented, and belligerent and even
assaultive when their organicity depends; the patient with
chronic organic brain syndrome secondary to arteriosclerotic
vascular disease who becomes violent at night in the nursing
home is the commonest example of this. Along these lines,
incidentally, it is necessary to point out that the controversy surrounding the role of epilepsy and aggression has

to do with the causal role between brain dysfunction such as
psychomotor epilepsy and violence and it is not at all
clear from scientific evidence whether violence can spring
from a psychomotor seizure or whether it instead results
from the post-ictal confusional state which often follows
such seizures (Rodin, 1973). Thus, in this area also we
may be dealing with an altered sensorium which gives rise
to belligerent and combative behavior.

A final group of patients are those who demonstrate violence
as a result of psychosocial circumstances, and I refer here
to a wide variety of clinical behaviors ranging from the
adolescent who is in turmoil and behaves belligerently to
the man who hits the gas station attendant because he cannot
obtain gas. As always in such social situations, the pre-
morbid personality patterns play a role and some individuals
are more prone than others to hit and swing instead of
react passively and with acquiescence. This is, of course,
true with the organic brain syndromes also: the paranoid,
belligerent man may become more paranoid and more belligerent when his sensorium is impaired. The point I am
trying to make, however, is that aggressive behavior may
have strong social precipitants which make experimental
simulation difficult.

The difficulty of reproducing violent behavior in the
laboratory is compounded by the problem of psychodynamics.
By this I mean the particuar psychologic status of the
individual who is violent or prone to violence and whose
violence is triggered off by rather predictable psychologic
stresses such as abandonment or insults to sexual role.
For example, in my work with violent prone patients I have
found abandonment to be a key stress on a patient and
lead him to react with aggression. For example, I had a
patient who became homicidal when his wife left him, and
this abandonment triggered off a childhood memory of rage
stemming from maternal abandonment. In psychotherapy, we
worked on this issue profitably. The point here is: how
would one replicate such a psychodynamic pattern in the
laboratory? A medical student in my clinic has produced a
series of videotapes with specific psychodynamic themes:
helplessness, abandonment, homosexuality, and the like and
we show these to patients to get them talking about their
conflicts. We do not, however, show these films to

patients in order to get them angry or aggressive though I
imagine one might be able to do this and devise a set of
psychological stressors that would activate the patient to
violence, much as certain stressful films change GSR or other
psychophysiologic measures.

I should like to talk briefly about guns, alcohol, and
victims because they play a key role in violence in man.
Violence among humans occurs among intimates (Goode, 1969),
among people who know each other because people who know
each other can hurt each other, emotionally speaking.
Stranger-to-stranger violent crimes are comparatively rare,
though increasing in this country. Given that crimes of
violence occur among intimates, it has become apparent to
workers in the field of criminology (Macdonald, 1961) that
the victim may be a responsible party to the assailant's
actions and we, too, have observed the provocative role that
victims may play in a violent act. I have heard stories of
wives daring their husbands to pull the trigger and participated in a number of forensic cases where the murder was
just the natural outcome of a heritage of familial violence
with guns lying around the household freely waiting to be
used. It is even recognized that the epidemiology of
aggravated assault and homicide is basically the same; the
difference would appear to reside only in the availability of
a weapon which is as deadly as a gun (Pikorny, 1965). The
instrumental value of weapons is a factor of utmost importance in both individual violence and mass violence such as
war; needed research in the area of weapons and their
acquisition and use is lacking. Finally, alcohol is the drug
most clearly associated with violence both in terms of
violent crimes but also in driving fatalities where it
assumes a role in 30-50% of single car fatalities and an
equal role in violent crimes (Tinklenberg, 1973). Why this
should be so--why alcohol should predispose, if it does predispose, to violence is still unclear, despite voluminous
research literature in the field of alcoholism. I merely wish
to point out that alcohol is one variable which needs to be
taken account of when doing research on violence, as do the
roles of guns and victims. The point I am obviously trying to
make is that a violent act is not a clean cut affair in pure
culture. Therefore, replicating it in a laboratory is bound to
lead to oversimplification when work is done with humans.

I mentioned a moment ago automobile fatalities, and this
brings up the issue of which behavioral acts in humans to
consider violent. The American Psychiatric Association Task
Force on Clinical Aspects of the Violent Individual has
spent much effort in delineating which human acts are of
concern to a clinician and which should be labelled as
aggressive. For example, a soldier is violent but of course
need not see a psychiatrist unless his violence transcends
certain limits considered permissible by wartime standards
if war exists, or peacetime standards otherwise. I have
treated policemen who were considered violent by their
superiors, and such a behavior is a matter of much subjective
judgement; again, there is a thin dividing line between
what is useful and pathological violence (A.P.A. Task Force,
in press, 1974). There is also society's judgement regarding violence. For example, dangerous drivers are not yet
perceived by society as violent in the same sense as an
armed robber is, even though a group of dangerous recidivist
drivers could probably be identified if we put our minds to
it.

So far I have mentioned behavior; there are other violent
patients who psychiatrists see who have not yet been
violent but the problem is to predict their potential for
violence. These patients are often mistakenly labelled as
dangerous, a legal term which is perjorative and may
unfortunately justify incarceration. I should like to deal
with the issue of dangerous simply by saying that there is
a large literature on this field bu no one test or group
of psychological tests or set of human qualities which have
been shown to be more predictive of human characteristics
when follow up studies are done. Harry Kozol (1972) a
psychiatric worker in this field at the Center for Dangerous
Persons in Bridgewater, a Massachusetts Correctional Agency,
has said that the best "predictor" of violence is still a
feeling on the part of the clinician that the patient is
cold, irreverant of human life, aloof, and emotionally
distant. These are subjective parameters, and give those
of us in the business of making clinical statements about
patients little solace. But it is perhaps as it should be,
for we often lack humility in this matter of deciding who
is dangerous and who is not. The point is again that the
matter of defining and predicting who is aggressive and
who is not is complex and arduous; it is as difficult as the

prediction of any other human trait, like courage, fortitude, or altruism. When one predicts capacity for aggression one is not predicting the occurrence of a disease entity such as depression or psychosis which has, as I have mentioned, clearer clinical characteristics.

By the way, many patients come to me with fantasies of doing harm and no history of violence. They are afraid of going out of control and injuring someone or fear their own potential explosiveness directed against spouses or children. The problem is not violent behavior, but violent ideation and violent thoughts. Most people who are violent, even impulsive ones, can feel their anger building up to some extent. With psychosomatic patients, the anger becomes somatically bound and hence often detectable; with paranoid and even obsessional patients, there is some degree of "signal" anxiety, and even with the Explosive Personality, some vague warning signs occur in the way of bodily sensations such as tightening of the stomach or a headache. Indeed, with such patients, therapy is heavily weighted toward alerting them to the premonitory signs and symptoms which accompany violent outbursts so that they can become aware, ahead of time, that they are angry rather than explode (Lion, 1972). But I shall talk about this further in a moment. Now, I am drawing attention to the phenomenology of aggression in man and making the point that violence is perceived in the mind and the body before it becomes translated into assaultive or destructive behavior. In fact, many aggressive patients have an impoverished initial ability to fantasize and affectively realize that they are angry so that, prior to treatment, they spill over their anger into behavior without being able to talk about it and recognize the nature of their feelings. This matter of recognizing aggressive affect lends itself to research strategies in humans.

I move now to the area of treatment of aggression in man. The areas to be covered are the psychotherapeutic, pharmacologic, and somatic methods of treatment.

I have already alluded to some principles in the psychotherapy of aggression in man. Aggressive patients are generally very defensive and constantly exert emotional energy to protect a weak, fragile inner core of vulnera-

bility.   This is particularly the case with the more
paranoid individuals who are always on guard for attack and
who attack at the slightest provocation. Many aggressive men
are sensitive to slurs on masculinity and threatened by any
kind of passivity or posture of helplessness and the therapy
in such cases must ultimately come to grips with the inner
insecurity which propels these patients on their relentless
need to be defensive. Other patients present with super-
masculine stances of the so often recognizable reaction
formation against any insults against family members which
bespeaks rage and hatred at, say, a depriving mother or
absent father. The psychotherapy of such patients, be it
individual or group is slow, time consuming, and difficult
due to the problems these patients have with intimacy,
trust, and the process of verbalization. In prison settings
such as Patuxent, Maryland, where an indeterminate sentence
is operative and where progress is contingent upon therapy,
the full range of defenses against insight and introspection
is readily apparent and one can only watch the painful and
slow procedure of self reflection, wishing that there were
some way to speed it up. It is a great inner emptiness and
sadness which is at the basis of these prisoners' need to be
powerful and strong and aggressive, and it is always easier
for them to be mad than sad. Like schizophrenics who emerge
through a depression before they relinquish their psychotic
mode of coping with reality; so, too the violent patient
must pass through a depressive phase of treatment before
he gains the strength to be weak, though that statement
sounds paradoxical (Lion, 1972).

It is perhaps more comfortable to move from the potent
though murky area of psychotherapy to the area of behavior
therapy (Yates, 1970). Assessment of psychotherapy and the
methodology of such assessment has plagued clinicians for
decades, but it is easier to get a baseline rate of
aggressive behavior and then determine the efficacy of the
behavior therapies in affecting violent actions. It is
this area which shows a great future research promise and
it is also this area which allows almost direct inter-
polation from animal and laboratory data to humans. For
example, paradigms of reinforcement have applicability to
certain human clinical situations in, for example, work
with retarded aggressive youngsters or disturbed, aggressive psychiatric patients.

Let me switch now to the pharmacology of aggression in man.
A wide variety of drugs have been advocated to control
violence in humans, including the major and minor tranquilizers, lithium, the anticonvulsants, CNS stimulants, and
hormonal analogs. The wide variety of drugs used attests,
of course, to the etiological diversity of aggression in
man. The literature on the subject of drugs in the treatment
of aggression is small, and will be forthcoming in a special
section in the Journal of Nervous and Mental Diseases (Lion
and Monroe, in press, 1974b). For now, I summarize the
rationales and indications for the various pharmacologic
agents. The major tranquilizers such as the phenothiazines,
thiothixenes, and butyrophenones have been stated to be
useful in treating aggression paritcularly when the aggression is part of a psychosis. Thus, the drugs may help by
their action on the thought disorder and there is actually
no drug of choice for aggression in this area. That is, one
or another antipsychotic agent may help the patient and the
clinician must try the various drugs out in some empirical
fashion. Some phenothiazines, for example, such as
chlorpromazine have a greater effect on the psychomotor
agitation than others. Other major tranquilizers such as
trifluoperazine are useful for "quieter" paranoid states
that can erupt into aggression.

The minor tranquilizers such as the benzodiazepines have
been stated to be useful in aggressive patients, though
they have no antipsychotic properties. It may be recalled
that early studies of chlordiazepoxide (Librium) and
oxazepam (Serax) on normal college volunteers showed some
of these drugs to increase aggression as measured on rating
scales (DiMascio, 1973). This disinhibitory effect has
been observed in the literature in clinical practice, but
I mention the studies to illustrate a particular point,
namely that drug effects in human research can involve
assessment through the use of rating scales and other
psychometric tests. The relevance of such tests to actual
"on-the-street" behavior may be highly questionable. In
any event, the benzodiazepines have usefulness in violent
patients, particularly the labile, impulsive personality
disorders I have previously described. Whether this is due
to their anticonvulsant properties or simply to their anti-
anxiety effects is unclear. The anticonvulsants such as
diphenylhydantoin have been touted as good for explosive

types of violent patients, though rigorous controlled
studies in the face of much positive publicity are sadly
lacking; indeed, there is more negative than positive literature on the usefulness of the drug diphenylhydantoin
(Dilantin) (Gottschalk et al, 1973). However, the drug
may help patients who demonstrate "ictal" forms of aggression which have been felt to represent subcortical epileptic
forms of behavior.

The CNS stimulants such as the amphetamines and methyl-
phenidates have been used with success in the treatment of
hyperkinetic syndromes and reduced the aggression present
in such syndromes. The mode of action of these drugs is
unclear and so we do not know precisely how the drug
influences behavior. Nor are we precisely clear how
experimental hormonal agents such as medroxy pregesterone
acetate works. This drug (Provera) still an experimental
agent has a direct CNS action as do all hormonal agents
(Money, 1970). For example, progesterone is an anesthetic
when administered intravenously and causes drowsiness. The
drug, of course, suppresses blood testosterone levels and so
we have some idea of the rationale and the pharmacology of
effect on patients with heightened sexual drive. I point
out to you that hormonal treatment has been studied in
animals, but the treatment of aggression in humans may be
qualitatively different (Kreuz and Rose, 1972). For example,
in the few patients I have treated with Provera as part of
a collaborative study with Johns Hopkins and Harvard, certain of these patients did indeed become less aggressive
but suffered from sleepiness, facial acne, certain body
changes, all rather small effects but of great psychological
impact, sufficient to jeopardize therapy. The point I am
making here is that drug effect on a target symptom may
not be enough when we are evaluating the psychopharmacologic
effect of the drug in humans.

Lithium is psychiatry's newest drug, and there are good
controlled studies showing the drug to be useful in
aggressive patients (Sheard, 1971). Why this is so remains
puzzling; the drug appears specific for a specific component
of a mood disorder; it may have some prophylactic value in
preventing depressions in manic-depressive disorders but
it certainly works with manics, including aggressive manics.
Why the drug should work on non-manic aggressive patients
is unclear. It is unlikely that it is due to any anti-

convulsant property since the antiepileptic effects of
lithium are still controversial.

I think it can be seen from the above discussion that there
is still little known about the site of action on the
various drugs which have been shown useful in the treatment
of aggression in man. Further, the drugs must be tried on
humans and on humans who have to work, drive a car, live in
a family, and so forth. To supress aggression is not enough;
for instance the drugs must be antiaggressive but not
sedative, just like antipsychotic agents should not be
sedative. It is my impression that we are unlikely to
discover one good antiaggressive agent in the future, because
the psychological etiologies of aggression are so varied
in man. It has often been said that a good antiaggressive
agent must localize in cortical or subcortical areas which
mediate or play a role in the expression of aggression in
man. Yet while the benzodiazepines have taming effects on
monkeys, their antiaggressive properties in humans are still
less than dazzling.

I shall only touch on the somatic therapies of aggression
in man. ECT remains useful for certain psychotic patients
with aggressiveness that is either life threatening or
refractory to medication. Castration has been used in
foreign countries to control hypersexually dangerous men;
its use has been supplanted by chemical methods of castration
which I have already mentioned. I should point out, by
the way, that among Sturup's series of 900 castrates, six
committed suicide (Sturup, 1968) so that there is reason to
be concerned about this somatic method of therapy in terms
of unexpected risks.

A wide range of neurosurgical procedures, including
temporal lobectomy, amydalectomy, cingulectomy, thalamotomy,
and hypothalamectomy have been used to control aggressive
epileptic patients refractory to medication and non-epileptic
patients with severe behavior problems. Serious methodological problems of preoperative assessment, criteria for
selection, indications for surgery, and follow-up have cast
much doubt on the efficacy and rationales for such procedures (Goldstein, 1974). This area of treatment, including
the amydalectomies in man has aroused great scientific
controversy and again brought to recognition the ethical

issues of suppressing violence in man by irreversible
destruction of brain tissue. Note that there are two
ethical issues here: the one I mentioned at the outset of
this paper--namely, the suppression of aggression versus
modulation (or giving the patient the opportunity to modulate
his own aggression) and the irreversibility of the therapy.
One may well be able to abolish a patient's aggressiveness
but the basic and haunting questions are: 1) what is the
price? and 2) when does one make that decision? How long do
we incarcerate a patient and try psychotherapy and behavior
therapy and all the drugs until we decide that the patient
needs some neurosurgical procedure to reduce aggression?
What risks do we take, and how do we measure the effects of
our intervention, for the measurement problem exists not
only with psychotherapy and drugs, but with surgery as well.
If one takes a patient who has three temper outbursts a week
and treats him, how do we determine the success of our
therapy? He may have fewer outbursts, or weaker outbursts,
or he may be rendered passive and docile. Who is a candi-
date for what therapy? Psychotherapy for a one-time
murderer seems reasonable, but what about the recidivist
rapist? How vigorous do we become in our treatment with
him, given the state of the art?

Few behaviors in man cause as many emotional reactions to
spectators as aggression (Lion, in press, 1974c). Aggression
is rooted in the origins of culture in this country; its
expression is a right. We own guns, we drive cars, we
drink.   And yet we continuously grapple with the problems
of penology and the problems effective penal reform.   It
happens that the prisons are filled with violent men and
yet we do not treat them because we don't know how and
really don't want to and we cannot forcibly try and treat
them because of concerns of a civil libertarians; even if
we would try, the whole area of human clinical research is
fast becoming impossible with new guidelines proposed by
governmental agencies, including NIH. If we are to further
our understanding of aggression in man and come to grips
with its phenomenology and treatment, we must work with
violent men and we must have populations of men who are
violent, not college volunteers who get mad at contrived
situations.   I urge scientists who work in the area of
violence to do some prison work or become acquainted with
patients who are violent, so that the animal and laboratory

models of aggresson more closely approach the violence which occurs on the street. In this way, the basic researcher can both help the clinician in learning basic science but also broaden his own understanding of the violence which occurs in man and is unique to man.

References

American Psychiatric Association Task Force on Clinical Aspects of the Violent Individual, Washington, D.C. (in press), 1974.

Arnold, L.E. Hyperkinetic adult: Study of the "paradoxical amphetamine response". J.A.M.A., 1972, 222, 693.

Bach-y-Rita, G., Lion, J.R., and Ervin, F.R. Pathological intoxication: Clinical and electroencephalographic studies. Amer. J. Psychiat., 1970, 127, 698.

Bach-y-Rita, G., Lion, J.R., Climent, C., and Ervin, F.R. Episodic dyscontrol: A study of 130 violent patients. Amer. J. Psychiat., 1971, 127, 1473.

Bandura, A., Ross, D., and Ross, S. Imitation of film-mediated aggressive model. J. Abnorm. Soc. Psychol., 1963, 66, 3.

Bromberg, W. Crime and the Mind. New York: Macmillan, 1965.

DiMascio, A. The effects of benzodiazepines on aggression: Reduced or increased? In The Benzodiazepines (S. Garattini, E. Mussini, and L.O. Randall, Eds.). New York: Raven Press, 1973, pp. 433.

Ellenwood, E.H. Assault and homicide associated with amphetamine abuse. Amer. J. Psychiat., 1971, 127, 1170.

Feshback, S. The stimulating versus cathartic effects of a vicarious aggressive activity. J. Abnorm. Soc. Psychol., 1961, 63, 381.

Gottschalk, L.A., Covi, L., Uliana, R., and Bates, D.E. Effects of diphenylhydantoin on anxiety and hostility in institutionalized prisoners. Comprhen. Psychiat., 1973, 14, 503.

Goldstein, M. Brain research and violent behavior. A
          summary and evaluation of the status of biomedical
          research on brain and aggressive violent behavior.
          Arch. Neurol., 1974, 30, 1.

Goode, W.J. Violence between intimates. In Crimes of
          Violence. National Commission on the Causes and
          Prevention of Violence Staff Study Series, Vol. 13,
          pg. 941, U.S. Gov't Print. Office, Washington, D.C.,
          1969.

Harticollos, P. The syndrome of minimal brain dysfunction
          in young adult patients. Bull. Menninger Clin., 1968,
          32, 102.

Kozol, H., Boucher, R.J., Garafalo, R.F. The diagnosis and
          treatment of dangerousness. Crime and Delinq., 1972,
          18, 371.

Kreuz, L.E. and Rose, R.M. Assessment of aggressive
          behavior and plasma testosterone in a young criminal
          population. Psychosomat. Med., 1972, 34, 321.

Lion, J.R. Evaluation and Management of the Violent
          Patient. Springfield, Illinois: Charles C. Thomas,
          1972.

Lion, J.R. The role of depression in the treatment of
          aggressive personality disorders. Amer. J. Psychiat.,
          1972, 129 347.

Lion, J.R. (Ed.). Personality Disorders: Diagnosis and
          Management. Baltimore: Williams and Wilkins, (in
          press), 1974a

Lion, J.R. On the development of a violence clinic. In The
          Violent Balance (S. Pasternak, Ed.). New York:
          Spectrum Publications, (in press), 1974c.

Lion, J.R., Bach-y-Rita, G., Ervin, F.R. Violent patients
          in the emergency room. Amer. J. Psychiat., 1969, 125,
          1706.

Lion, J.R., Azcarate, C., Christopher, R., and Arana, J.   A
        violence clinic. Maryland State Med. J., 1974, 23, 45.

Lion, J.R. and Monroe, R.R. (Eds.). Drugs in the Treatment
        of Aggression. (Special Section) J. Nerv. Ment. Dis.,
        (in press), 1974b.

Macdonald, J.M. The Murderer and His Victim. Springfield,
        Illinois: Charles C. Thomas, 1961.

Milgram, S. Behavioral study of obedience. J. Abnorm.
        Soc. Psychol., 1963, 67, 371.

Money, J. Use of an androgen depleting hormone in the
        treatment of male sex offenders. J. Sex. Research,
        1970, 6, 165.

Monroe, R.R. Episodic Behavioral Disorders. Cambridge:
        Harvard University Press, 1970.

Pokorny, A.D. Human violence: A comparison of homicide
        aggravated assault, suicide, and attempted suicide.
        J. Criminal Law, Criminology, and Police Science,
        1965, 56, 488.

Rodin, E.A. Psychomotor epilepsy and aggressive behavior.
        Arch. Gen. Psychiat., 1973, 28, 210.

Sheard, M.H. Effect of lithium in human aggression. Nature,
        1971, 230, 113.

Sturup, G.K. Treatment of sexual offenders in Herstedvester,
        Denmark. Acta Psychiat. Scan. Suppl., 1968, 204, 44.

Tinklenberg, J.R. Alcohol and Violence. In Alcoholism:
        Progress in Research and Treatment. New York:
        Academic Press, 1973.

Yates, A.J. Behavioral Therapy. New York: John Wiley,
        1970.

Plotnick: Do normal children respond to amphetamine like hyperkinetic children?

Penna: No, they respond like normal adults.

Miczek: You mentioned that among the various kinds of aggression you encounter as a clinician, a class of aggression induced by toxic states. The agents included LSD and amphetamine. Later you mentioned using amphetamine therapeutically. Would you comment on amphetamines duel roles.

Penna: The violence that one see in patients who have been abusing amphetamine is related to the psychotic state induced by the amphetamine. With the hyperkinetic child amphetamine has a paradoxical action, it calms. It was thought that when the child reaches puberty, this action would no longer take place. However, recently people have described adolescents and even adults who have shown a similar response. No one knows why the drug acts this way.

McGaugh: Are the effects of depressants, for example, barbituates, also paradoxical in the hyperkinetic child?

Penna: I do not think that is known because barbituates are not normally used with the hyperkinetic child.

Harvey: Children have a paradoxical response to many drugs, including depressant drugs, but to my knowledge hyperkinetic children respond to depressants like normal children. All depressants show a stimulant effect at low doses and children show this effect more than adults.

Miczek: Do you find any differences between acute and
                chronic drug effects?

Penna: That is difficult to answer because of individ-
                ual differences in drug response. For example,
                you may give a patient Valium; he may become
                agitated but only after a week or two weeks
                of usage, but I have seen this occurring even
                within one or two days.

Harvey: One of the problems in this area is that in
                very few of the studies do you have adequate
                controls. We need more double-blind studies.
                The placebo effect of drugs can be as high as
                65 per cent in double-blind studies. If it is
                not a double blind study it can go as high as
                90 per cent. Part of it is the response of
                the individual who knows that he is getting
                something that will help him and part of it
                the response of the observer who would like to
                see an effect. Another problem is that one can
                get opposite effects of drugs depending upon
                the setting.

ON AGGRESSIVE BEHAVIOR AND BRAIN DISEASE - SOME QUESTIONS AND POSSIBLE RELATIONSHIPS DERIVED FROM THE STUDY OF MEN AND MONKEYS[1]

Allan F. Mirsky[2]

and

Nancy Harman

Boston University

Boston, Massachusetts 02118

This paper addresses the issue of the relationship between violent or aggressive behavior and disease of the brain, and in particular focuses on the question of the relationship between epilepsy and pathological aggressive behavior. I should say at the outset that there are relatively few things that can be said with certainty in this area; for the most part there are a great many unanswered questions, but they are in large measure researchable. Hopefully we can spell out some of the dimensions of parameters of that research.

The paper will be divided into a number of sections: the first will concern the question of aggressive or violent behavior as an ictal act or epileptic equivalent; the next will concern the relation between the presence of an epileptiform disorder and "rude and overtly aggressive behavior", considered as an association of traits rather than as a behavioral manifestation

of some pathophysiological process; the third section will
concern the relation between the presence of an epileptiform
disorder and psychopathological behavior; the fourth section
will present some observations on the utility of subhuman primate models for gaining some insight into the problems in this
area; and the final section will present some proposals, both
modest and grandiose, for future studies.

Violent behavior as an ictal act. The belief that an individual act of violent or aggressive behavior can represent a
convulsive phenomenon stems from a number of sources. Modern
textbooks of neurology and psychiatry (Redlich and Freedman,
1966; Kolb, 1973) have lent currency to this belief, based
presumably upon clinical experience. Some modern polemics
(Mark and Ervin, 1970) and science-fiction works (Crichton,
1972) have also implicated temporal lobe disease, if not
temporal lobe epilepsy in the genesis of rage behavior. Moreover, the discussion of the recent famous cases of Jack Ruby
(Rodin, 1973) and other famous assassins and murderers (Sweet
et al., 1969) has referred to temporal lobe disease. The
notion is a plausible one from the viewpoint of the brain substrate presumably involved, since major portions of the limbic
system or visceral brain are either contained within the temporal lobe or are in direct anatomic relation with structures
within the temporal lobe. And since the limbic system is that
brain region or system thought to be necessary and responsible
for the maintenance and regulation of affective behavior,
disease in this system could lead to diseased behavior. Mark
and Ervin (1970) have presented what is perhaps the most
dramatic example of this in the book "Violence and the Brain"
in their description of the case of Julia. This young woman,
whose near-murderous rages were refractory to all kinds of
therapy, could be induced to perform violent acts upon stimulation of her presumably diseased amygdala. Her behavior is
reminiscent of the studies by Flynn and collaborators (1967) in
the cat and by Delgado and colleagues in the monkey (1967). In
these studies, aggressive behavior in social and quasi-social
contexts could be elicited by stimulation of the brain, although
not necessarily of the amygdala. In the present symposium Dr.
Perachio has provided some striking examples of this behavior
in the monkey. However, despite the compelling nature of the
example of Julia, and the interesting examples provided by
Flynn, Delgado and Perachio, the bulk of evidence suggests that
ictal rage or violence in men is a very rare phenomenon. In a

symposium similar to the present one, reported in 1967, Pierre
Gloor, Chief of Electroencephalography at the Montreal Neurological Institute, made the following statement: "It is well
known that in animal experiments behavioral patterns suggesting
fear and aggression, as well as opposite states suggestive of
rewarding emotions, can be elicited from stimulation within
the amygdaloid complex. It would therefore be reasonable to
expect all these various emotional states to be part of the
repertoire of symptoms that may be engendered by excessive
discharge in the amygdaloid region in cases of temporal lobe
or psychomotor epilepsy. Although this undoubtedly is true in
a very general way, it is nevertheless surprising that, in the
overwhelming majority of patients who experience an ictal
emotion, this emotion is fear. All other emotions, such as
anger, sorrow, pleasure or elation appear only in very rare
and isolated cases. Rage, with or without aggressive behavior,
is an extremely rare ictal phenomenon. Furthermore, I would
suspect that some, perhaps even the reported cases of ictal
rage, would not withstand a critical assessment of the evidence.
Frequently, aggressive behavior associated with a fit is not
at all an ictal, but rather a postictal phenomenon, elicited
in the postictal confusional state. This often occurs because
the patient is restrained by well-meaning people in an attempt
to protect him. In addition, however, temporal lobe epileptics
frequently display sudden outbursts of anger, generally
triggered by minor provocations. But these are not seizures,
nor do these outbursts generally occur in close relationship
with seizure; I myself, have never seen an instance of true
ictal rage (emphasis added). In our experience at the Montreal
Neurological Institute we have never produced rage or anger as
a response to temporal lobe stimulation in patients undergoing
surgical treatment for their seizures. On the other hand, it
is very common to elicit fear by such stimulation" (Gloor, 1967,
p. 118). Gloor, nevertheless, went on to describe an epileptic
patient whose outbursts of rage and assaultive behavior (as
well as his seizures) were ameliorated by removal of a portion
of his diseased right temporal lobe. Gloor was careful to
state, however, that the relationship between amelioration of
seizures and of pathological behavior was complex, and that
there were sufficient instances of one occurring without the
other to suggest that the "relationship is certainly not a
simple one." Other studies bear this out (Mark and Ervin, 1970;
Falconer et al., 1958; Blumer, 1967; Serafetinides, 1965).

A recent study by Rodin (1973) confirms Gloor's experience and statement on the nonoccurrence of ictal rage. He reports on a series of 150 seizure cases seen in the Lafayette Clinic, including 42 with psychomotor automatisms as an ictal event. All had seizures induced by bemegride for diagnostic purposes and were photographed during this time. "There was no instance of ictal or postictal aggressive behavior in this study; when there was danger of aggressive behavior, it could promtly be averted by abandoning restraint efforts" (Rodin, 1973, p. 210). Rodin also reported that of 700 unselected seizure patients seen in their clinic, only 34 (4.8%) were found in which the variable "destructive-assaultive" had been coded in their computer processed medical record forms. One has perhaps no way of getting a relevant figure for a control population, but the incidence of violent behavior seems surprisingly low.

An earlier study by Ajmone Marsan and Ralston (1957) provides further evidence. In this work, 153 metrazol-induced seizures in 119 patients were analyzed, including 92 convulsions in 69 patients with diagnoses of temporal lobe epilepsy. The sole mention of any behavior related to aggressiveness or violence is the following passage: "Restlessness and agitated behavior: This finding is also fairly common in the post-ictal period following a generalized attack (40% of seizures). Patients will thrash about, fumble with clothes, try to get up and remove electrodes. It is extremely unusual for them to show any hostility, especially if unrestrained at this time (emphasis added). However, as it is necessary to preserve electrode contacts for post-ictal recording and to keep the patient awake for testing, agitated behavior is not infrequently seen, and may occasionally require sedation. Unlike post-ictal chewing, it seems to have no preferential distribution in the various diagnostic groups" (Ajmone Marsan and Ralston, 1957, p. 117).

Specifically with reference to epileptic automatisms, Gunn and Fenton (1972) studied a group of 43 patients from a clinic population of 434 who showed a "condition of impaired awareness in which an individual may perform a series of actions of complex kind, the degree of awareness varying insofar as there may subsequently be complete amnesia to the incident or, if it can be recalled, recollection is imprecise and partial." The authors concluded that acts of violence are unusual in the context of an automatism, that the latter has little role in crime,

and further that the "present data indicate that the excess
prevalence of epilepsy discovered in the prison population
cannot be explained in terms of automatic behavior."

Although this survey is undoubtedly not exhaustive, it seems
sufficiently comprehensive to suggest that ictal rage, whether
associated with temporal lobe disease, temporal lobe automatisms or not, is sufficiently rare to be considered either a
curiosity or, perhaps a non-existent phenomenon. And further,
that the production of aggressive attack behavior by brain
stimulation in experimental animal subjects is not a model for
the clinical seizure phenomena seen in man.

Aggressive and rude behavior and epilepsy. Although the evidence of the existence of ictal rage is scant, there does
exist a body of data, gathered in the course of surveys and
clinical series both medical and neurosurgical, that suggests
"that patients with temporal lobe epilepsy are usually prone
to mental disorders and that amongst these disorders overtly
aggressive and rude behavior is the most common single entity"
(Taylor, 1969). Whether or not there is an association with
mental disorders is a separate issue and will be treated as
such; however the question of enhanced aggressivity can be
considered independently. It is not the intention here to
review all of the clinical literature relating to this phenomenon; however, it should be noted that attention to the issue
really begins with the practical development of the electro-
encephalogram in the late 1930's, which permitted and facilitated localization of epileptic disorders in various regions of
the cerebrum. A considerable contribution has been made by
neurologists and alienists from Great Britain, and many of the
relevant studies have been provided by or encouraged by such
men as Hill, Falconer, Ounsted, Pond, Serafetinides and their
colleagues. Somewhat more recently researchers in the United
States including Sweet, Mark, Ervin, Lion, Blumer and others
have begun to contribute both data and theorizing to the
questions of the etiology and management of aggressive-violent
behavior in temporal lobe disease.

Despite the conclusion reached by Taylor, cited above, there is
little unanimity of view that temporal lobe disease and violence
are related. An N.I.N.D.S. panel recently concluded: "Epilepsy
appears to be a rare "cause" for violent and aggressive behavior.
Although there is some difference in the reported association

between temporal lobe epilepsy and violent behavior, most
neurologists believe that the relationship is equal to or only
slightly higher than in the nonepileptic population"
(Goldstein, 1974, p. 32).

The conclusions of the N.I.N.D.S. panel notwithstanding i.e.,
that epilepsy is a rare cause of violence, there are a number
of studies suggesting that there is significant association
between temporal lobe disease and aggressive behavior. The
proportion of aggressive persons among epileptics may not be
greater than in the population at large, but when an epileptic
is identified as being aggressive, violent or having a "conduct
disorder", then the chances are, apparently, that he will have
a temporal lobe focus. It must be emphasized here that this
is a tentative statement since not all the published material
supports it (e.g., Stevens, 1966; Gibbs, 1952; Gunn and Bonn,
1970); what is needed is a very good, large scale survey.
However, among temporal lobe cases who are so ill as to require
surgical relief of their seizures, the proportion of those
who display some kind of an aggressiveness (ranging from "conduct disorders" to "catastrophic rage") is reported to be
approximately 1/3. This statement too, must be qualified.
Since most of this literature is British, and since British
neurosurgeons (e.g. Falconer) may be quasi-psychosurgical in
their approach (more so, say than Canadian surgeons such as
Penfield and Rasmussen) it is conceivable that those patients
selected for neurosurgical relief of seizures in Great Britain
are more likely to have behavioral problems in addition to their
convulsive symptoms. Notwithstanding these complications, the
literature suggests that a certain pattern or syndrome can be
identified in those seizure patients having behavior problems.
They have the following characteristics:
1.   They tend to be of the male sex.
2.   They tend to come from lower class socioeconomic back-
      grounds.
3.   Their abnormality tends to be localized in the left
      temporal lobe, although there is less unanimity as
      to whether the focus is anterior or posterior.[3]
4.   The onset of seizures tends to occur at a younger age
      than in subjects who are not behavior problems.
5.   There is a higher incidence in such persons, of dis-
      turbed family backgrounds, psychosis in near-relatives
      and periods spent in institutions such as reform
      schools and training schools.

This characterization is based on the studies of Taylor (1969);
Rey, Pond and Evans (1949); Hill (1953); Serafetinides (1965);
Ounsted (1969); and Grunberg and Pond (1957). However, not
every study has reported every finding. Any theory or
theoretically-oriented treatment approach to this issue should
try to take these findings into account, in order to produce
the correct equation with appropriate weights for the several
variables that have been implicated. In my view, no theoretical account of these matters that has been published is
completely satisfactory, although some appear wiser and more
comprehensive than others. Some of the hypotheses that have
been offered are listed in Table 1, somewhat paraphrased for
purposed of contrast and clarity.

The table is an attempt to characterize the unique interpretation made by the several students of the problem listed
above; most make at least passing reference to social and
familial factors, as well, in the genesis of the disorder.
We find the first three hypotheses most compatible with our
own thinking, emphasizing as they do a multidetermined etiology
which encompasses (in addition to the life-long stress of
seizures) defective cognitive mechanisms of long standing
(these are well described by Milner, 1962) possible social
class differences in the acceptability of aggressive acts, and
the accumulated anger and frustration derived from an impoverished, punishing and perhaps painful childhood. The "immaturity" stressed in hypothesis one is not completely convincing,
for angry behavior in infants or children does not seem to be
identical (except superficially) with that seen in aggressive
adults. With respect to the cognitive defects noted above, it
is perhaps worthy of emphasis that a person with temporal lobe
disease (especially of the left side) may have considerable
difficulty in communicating with and relating to others verbally.
In addition to contributing to continual academic failure, it
may be a source of interpersonal inadequacy and frustration.
There is the additional complication of trying to cope with
growing up, while at the same time functioning (or attempting
to function) under heavy medication. Possibly, for such persons,
physical aggression may be the last recourse by which one
expresses feelings of great intensity. One wonders also,
whether the catastrophic rage or violence described in some
patients may be understood as a means of warding off catastrophic feelings of anxiety, inadequacy or worthlessness.

TABLE 1

Hypotheses that have been offered to account for greater

incidence of aggressive behavior in epileptic patients,

especially those with temporal lobe foci

1. Immaturity: Due to early injury, there is a defect in
    maturation of temporal lobe structures (they are like
    those of a child) and an attendant defect in physiological
    (EEG) and behavioral functions (control of anger, verbal
    ability, I.Q.) dependent on this part of the brain (Rey,
    Pond and Evans, 1949).

2. Learning defect plus environmental stress: Because of the
    damage, there is a defect in learning or adjustment; this
    is exacerbated by poor social and familial background
    (Taylor, 1969; Serafetinides, 1965).

3. Seizures plus environmental stress: The stress of seizures,
    both within the person and within the family, coupled with
    adverse social and familial factors lead to conduct dis-
    orders (Note: Not restricted to temporal lobe epilepsy)
    (Grunberg and Pond, 1957).

4. Lack of cortical inhibition: The normal cortical inhibitory
    effects on the amygdala - hypothalamic (VM) circuit are
    absent, leading to unchecked rage. This can be corrected
    by lesioning of the amygdala (Walker and Blumer, 1974).

5. Hidden Seizures: There may be occult seizure activity
    somewhere in the limbic system, undetected in the scalp
    (or cortical) EEG. The expression of this may be a
    violent act. The buildup of subjective tension prior to
    such an act is reminiscent of that seen prior to a con-
    vulsion (Note: Such patients may show few overt signs of
    epilepsy, temporal lobe or otherwise!) (Sweet, Mark and
    Ervin, 1969).

Goldstein (1951) has described the latter as the sequela of impairment in the abstract attitude, which is in his view an inevitable consequence of cerebral damage in man.

Hypotheses four and five are essentially physiological, and in their purest form gross oversimplifications. Hypothesis five, at least, has the virtue of ultimately being testable. Conceivably this could be the true description of intracerebral events in a relatively small number of cases, although the evidence reviewed in the first section renders it unlikely, and suggests that it must be extremely rare. We shall return to some of these questions in the last section.

Epileptic disorders and psychopathology. Aside from the issue of aggressive behavior, there is a long tradition of belief that there is an association between epileptic disorders of the temporal lobe and psychiatric disorder. The chief architect of this belief is Frederic Gibbs, who in a number of publications (e.f. Gibbs & Gibbs, 1952) based upon the study of thousands of cases of epilepsy reported that the incidence of psychiatric symptoms (ranging from lethargy to psychosis) in cases of temporal lobe disease is about 45 - 55%. By contrast, in patients with other epileptogenic foci, the incidence of such symptoms is on the order of 10%. (In passing, it may be noted that Gibbs reports that the indicence of temper tantrums, rage attacks and assaultive tendencies combined in cases of psychomotor epilepsy is no more than 3 - 4%).

Gibbs makes clear that he views the epileptic and psychiatric symptoms as quite separable entities, since they may respond differentially to medication (seizures may improve whilst behavior worsens). These are not ictal disorders, but the consequence of the pathological involvement of an important brain area which has a major responsibility in his view for sensation, perception, evaluation and judgement. It is the impairment of these faculties, concomitant with temporal lobe disease, which gives rise to the behavior disturbances. (It is of interest that Gibbs makes no mention of subcortical or limbic pathology in his account; this is unusual among students of this problem).

Although the documentation with large numbers of cases is not present, essentially the same view (i.e., of the relation between temporal lobe disease and psychiatric disorder) is shared by another eminent epileptologist, Denis Hill (1953).

However, these conclusions are not supported by all investigators. Janice Stevens (1966) has made the point that when statistics are gathered by toting patients and symptoms into various categories without matching groups, then one may reach erroneous conclusions. In a series of studies by Stevens and her associates and admirers (Stevens, 1966; Mirsky et al., 1960; Small, Small and Hayden, 1966), the difference between temporal lobe and control epileptic populations in the incidence of psychiatric disease or symptoms virtually vanishes. However, epileptic patients as a group may show higher incidences of psychiatric illness than general medical patients. This may be a function of growing up epileptic, rather than being associated with any specific pathology. In the first of these publications, Stevens reviews the findings of a number of other investigators which have shed doubt on the temporal lobe – psychopathology association. A particular point which she makes is that patients with temporal lobe illness tend to be more similar in the distribution of ages to those hospitalized for psychosis in the general population than are other epileptics. Consequently, failure to match patients by age can suggest an artifactual relation of temporal lobe disease to psychiatric disorder.

There is, unfortunately, no clear and simple statement that can be made about the relation between the two entities under discusssion. There are undoubtedly substantial numbers of patients to be found with concurrent temporal lobe and psychiatric disease; however, whether temporal lobe disease, or epilepsy per se is the etiologic agent, and by what mechanisms, appears largely unknown. The issue, on the basis of the literature, at least, appears to be very much in doubt and in order to be resolved would require much more information than is currently available.

On the utility of monkey research in the study of temporal lobe functions: One may question the reason for inclusion of this material in a paper concerned with the relation between aggressive and violent behavior and temporal lobe disease in man. The justification is provided by the fact that the classic, seminal work of Klüver and Bucy (1939) is quoted by virtually every author in this field, and in particular by those who wish

to argue that surgery of the temporal lobes may have a beneficial effect on disordered behavior in man, whether or not
there is demonstrable pathology of the temporal lobes (Sweet,
Ervin and Mark, 1969).

As is well known, Klüver and Bucy described a variety of
behavioral changes in monkeys following bilateral removal of
primarily the anterior portions of the temporal lobes in
monkeys. The change of most interest, perhaps, for the present
discussion is the "taming" effect (referring to reduced
aggressiveness towards the human observer). The social behavior of the operated animals vis á vis other monkeys appears
considerably distorted. Other changes which have stimulated
great interest have been the hypersexuality, increased oral
tendencies and impaired visual abilities. At the outset it
must be noted that on the whole the surgery of the temporal
lobes did not do the experimental subjects very much good, and
their lot from the time of surgery to the time they reached
the hands of the histologist was not a happy one. We believe
that this is important to emphasize. Consideration only of
the "taming" produced by the Klüver and Bucy procedure
(ignoring the other potentially disastrous effects) has, in
part, served to stimulate several neurosurgeons to remove portions of the temporal lobe (or structures within it) in man
to reduce aggressive or psychotic behavior (Mark and Ervin,
1970; Chapman, 1958; Chitanondh, 1966; Balasubramanian and
Ramamurthi, 1970; Narabayashi, 1963; Scoville and Milner, 1957).
(One wonders whether Professor Klüver may feel something of
the emotions that Dr. Einstein felt on viewing photographs of
Hiroshima!) Clearly, the sole justification for this procedure,
on the basis of the original Klüver and Bucy work, was that it
might make a patient easier to manage, but not that it would
necessarily produce on the whole a beneficial change for the
patient.

Since the amygdala is the structure within the temporal lobe
which has received the most surgical and experimental attention,
it seems appropriate to review some of what is known about the
relation between this structure and social behavior, as revealed
by monkey studies, and to suggest what might still be learned.
Our original study (Rosvold, Mirsky and Pribram, 1954) has been
reviewed often and need not be discussed here in detail. Briefly,
when we operated ad seriatim the three most dominant members of

a monkey social group (Figure 1), we found dramatic losses in dominance in the first two animals (Figures 2 and 3) but not in the third. The second animal operated (Zeke) remained dominant over the first to be operated (Dave) who previously had been the alpha animal in the group. Therefore, it was clear that amygdala lesions did not necessarily eliminate inter-animal aggressive behavior, although they might reduce dominance rank. Although the number of aggressive acts and dominance rank are correlated, they are separate measures. The third animal (Riva) showed no fall in dominance behavior, and impressed us as being more aggressive post surgery than prior to it (Figure 4). Two additional observations are worthy of note: despite the variability in the group or social cage results, all animals showed increased tameness (or reduced fear) towards the human observer after surgery. It is questionable, however whether this is a specific result of amygdala damage, since the same "taming" effect was seen following cingulate lesions (Mirsky, Rosvold and Pribram, 1957) and hippocampal lesions (Mirsky, 1960). With these lesions at least, the taming seems to dissipate with time and our impressions were that even amygdalectomized animals were indistinguishable in their home cages from normal animals after several months.

The second observation is that the two animals who did fall in dominance (Dave and Zeke) had larger lesions in the basolateral portion of the amygdala than did Riva. Therefore, in addition to the host of other variables that may be involved in interpreting the variability of our results (i.e., differing group structure following each animal's lesion, differing lengths of time the group had been together, etc.) there is an additional anatomic variable that has never been studied systematically. One study that we did launch following this early work attempted to address the issue of variability in postoperative experience as a determinant of the outcome of surgery. Three animals, each of which occupied a middle position in a social group, were subject to bilateral amygdala lesions. After surgery, they were given dominance "training": they were placed for six weeks with groups of small, young animals whom they could easily dominate. On return to their original social groups none showed a fall in dominance; one rose one rank in the hierarchy permanently, and one showed the same change on a temporary basis. All showed increased instances of aggressive acts towards those below them

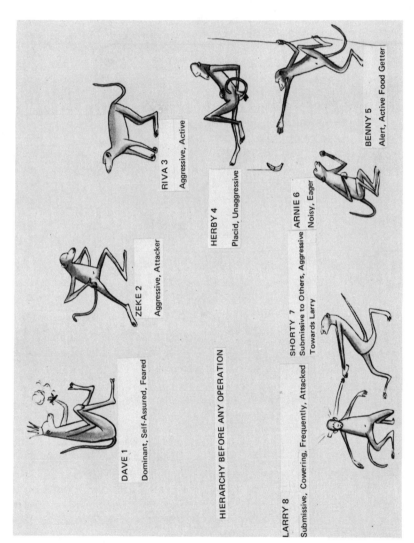

Figure 1. Dominance hierarchy observed in a group of eight adolescent male monkeys. This was determined on the basis of several months of daily observation in a competitive feeding situation, including several periods of separation for individual-cage housing and observation and reconstitution of the group.

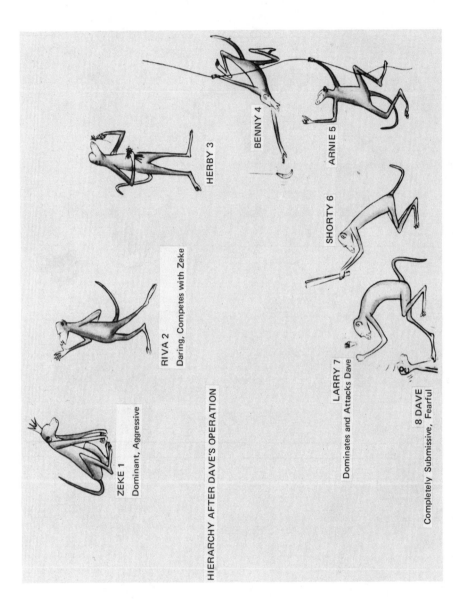

Figure 2. Dominance hierarchy after bilateral amygdala lesions in Dave; note drop of Dave from most dominant to least dominant rank, and intactness of balance of hierarchy.

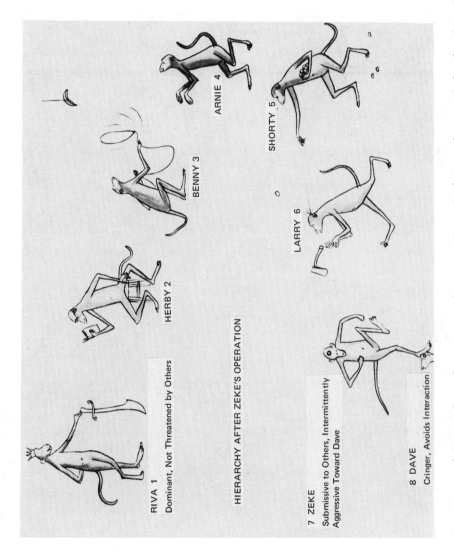

Figure 3. Dominance hierarchy after second operation; bilateral amygdala lesion in Zeke. Although submissive to other animals, Zeke remained dominant and aggressive towards Dave.

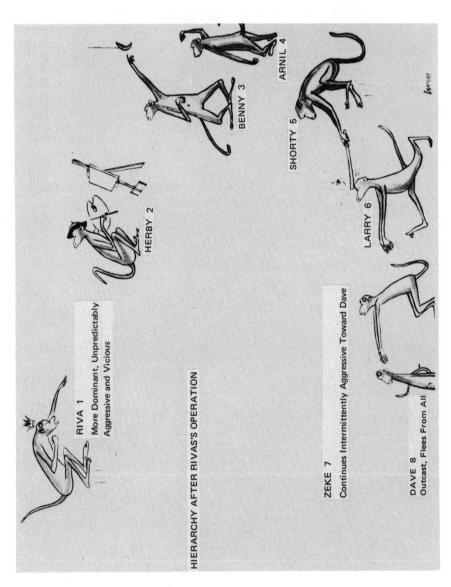

Figure 4.   Dominance hierarchy after bilateral amygdala lesion in Riva. He appeared more aggressive after surgery. No other changes in dominance rank were observed.

in the dominance hierarchy (Figure 5). Control animals, who had neither surgery nor the exposure to young animals, showed no such changes. This experiment bears replication, with all the appropriate control groups; at the least, however, it casts additional doubt on the immutable relation between "tameness" and amygdala lesions. What was suggested instead was that such a lesion might weaken learned associations between stimuli and reinforcers and produce a plastic state whereby new behaviors might be instituted (Mirsky, 1960).

I do not wish to imply that no other research on the relation-ship between temporal lobe structures and social behavior has been conducted in the last fifteen years. Kling and assoc-iates (1970, 1972), Plotnik (1968), and Franzen and Myers (1972) to name some examples, have contributed interesting work, including the dramatic demonstration that amygdalectomy in the free-ranging vervet monkey renders it totally unable to cope with its normal habitat; such animals perish within a short time (Kling, Lancaster and Benitone, 1970)[4]. The point I wish to make is that we have at this time primarily a series of dramatic, or interesting, or puzzling observations, but no fundamental penetration of the problem. Our understanding of the behavioral effects of amygdala lesions, the area(s) of the amygdala which are critical for behavioral change, and the interaction between lesions and experience is quite limited. It is so limited in fact that there is no justification on the basis of animal studies to have performed amygdalotomy on a single human patient. Nevertheless, more than 500 cases have already had such surgery (Goldstein, 1974) presumably because there was sufficient justification on the basis of other cri-teria. The results are usually difficult to interpret, in part because neurosurgeons are not the best equipped persons to evaluate the behavioral effects of their procedures (Poppen, cited by Valenstein, 1973).

Proposals for future studies. The intent of this meeting was not simply to provide another review of research in the area of aggressive behavior, but to focus on what appear to be the important unsolved but soluble problems. The questions of the relationship between epileptic illness and behavior pathology, of the influence of specific brain lesions on social and adaptive behavior and of the remediation of neurologic and behavioral disorders are of continuing interest to neuro-

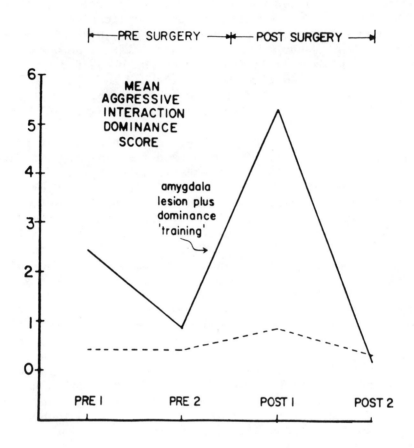

Figure 5.   Dominance scores (mean aggressive interaction
             tallies) for amygdala-lesioned animals with "domi-
             nance training" (See text for explanation). These
             animals showed increased aggressiveness in the
             first post-op period. Control animals (dashed line)
             without lesions and dominance training, but who were
             separated from the group for the same period of time,
             showed no significant changes in aggressive inter-
             action scores or in dominance rank. 7

scientists. Our hope is that continued careful scientific
work and scholarly attention to these questions will eventually
lead to enhanced understanding of brain-behavior relations,
and better methods of treatment and prevention of neurological
and behavioral illness. I think that we should oppose crash
programs aimed at eliminating violence, eradicating epilepsy
(or schizophrenia) or similar goals because I do not believe
those problems are susceptible to that kind of approach. They
require instead careful, systematic, adequately funded research
where one good idea matures and seeds others. Further, when
crash programs fail to yield the hoped-for "answers" in five
years or ten, the disillusionment among those who provide the
funds is great and the effects on research can be devastating.
But what can be done now that is not being done, that could
help attain the goals of better understanding, care and prevention of illness in the areas we have discussed? I am very
impressed by the national health registries that exist in many
European (and in particular Scandinavian) countries. If such
existed in our country then we would have an enormous resource
that could be used to study, survey and plan for all the health
needs of our country, in addition to the ones relevant to
today's discussion. At the least we should have a national
registry of persons with convulsive illnesses, so that all of
the 2,000,000 (or is it 4,000,000?) patients so afflicted in
the United States would be known. Such a repository of information could include a great deal of census-type data so that
the relation between convulsive illness and demographic factors
could be appreciated. If the standard reporting forms were to
include reliable and valid indices of behavioral as well as
neurological pathology, then the questions as to the relationship between temporal lobe disease and aggressive behavior
could be answered in a truly satisfactory way, and perhaps for
the first time. The neurologic information would have to be
high quality as well. This might require training many additional neurologists or enhancing the training of other medical
practitioners. It may well be that the current movement
towards Health Maintenance Organizations and Comprehensive
Epilepsy Centers will facilitate the establishing of a national
registry, but it would seem to be of high priority that the
needs of researchers would be kept in mind while these programs
are still in the planning stages. Some areas of the country
already have made a start in this direction, although the total
amount of useful behavioral data contained in existing reposi-

tories is probably quite limited. The experience of those who
were involved with the N.I.N.D.S. Collaborative Perinatal
Study could be enlisted to try to insure the success of this
enterprise.

What I am suggesting, therefore, is that only large scale
survey data with competent, standardized reporting of neurologic, psychiatric and behavioral information will permit us
to describe adequately the relation between epilepsy, temporal
lobe disease and disordered social behavior. I believe it
relatively unfruitful to continue to do small, possibly biased-
sample studies without adequate controls for the variables
which have already been shown to have been implicated: age,
social class, cognitive capacities, adequacy of educational
and family experience, severity of illness and locus of
lesion. I believe that I realize the potential cost of what
I am proposing but I promised that some of the recommendations
would be grandiose. And the potential additional information
that would be provided for planning and research purposes
would insure the value of the project. For example, if an
association were found between aggressive, violent or other
socially unacceptable behavior and a series of other neurologic,
demographic and environmental variables, then a prospective
study could be undertaken in which a group of infants or young
children at risk for such complications in later life could
be extended every possible medical, environmental and social
benefit. A matched control group without such advantages
would be constituted that would not receive such comprehensive
ministrations, and the outcome of the two groups could be
evaluated at 5, 10 and 15 years. If the treatment were
successful in preventing or reducing the development of
unacceptable behavior, it could then be extended, hopefully,
to all children at risk.

Some other suggestions of somewhat less utopian and grandiose
nature follow. The mysterious and possibly insubstantial
relationship between ictal events and aggressive behavior is
troubling; perhaps ictal rage never or rarely occurs in hospital
because the patient feels more secure and relaxed and hence less
anxious. It is a common experience that many patients have
fewer seizures while in a hospital. Possibly, the phenomenon
should be studied á la family therapy, i.e., observe family
groups who are maintained in a residence within an institution.

These family groups would include an epileptic member whose EEG can be monitored more or less continuously with telemetric methods. Such information would not speak to the issue of occult limbic seizures, but on balance the information might be worth gathering.

The questions concerning the role of the amygdala and other limbic structures in social-affective behavior appear to be too difficult to approach in human subjects, at least with existing technology. However, I believe that we have much to learn from monkey social groups, in which the developmental, experiential and neural variables can be controlled and manipulated with great precision. I would be particularly eager to see careful behavioral dissection of the nuclear groups within the amygdala, perhaps combined with the kind of pre- and postoperative environmental manipulation to which I have alluded. This could be extended to other limbic and neocortical structures, as well. I am not convinced of the necessity of conducting such studies under completely free-ranging conditions; in fact this may be detrimental, since some animal preparations do not survive. Laboratory and semi-field conditions would be adequate, if not superior, for the purposes I have described. I believe that we owe Klüver and Bucy and the 500 plus amygdalotomized patients no less than to discover what the role of the amygdala in social-affective behavior really is.

FOOTNOTES

[1] Supported in part by N.I.M.H. Grant MH-12568.

[2] Research Scientist Award, N.I.M.H., K3-MH14915.

[3] The increased incidence of left vs. right sided abnormalities
might be related to the most common presentation of the fetus
in utero during delivery. Thus, Ajmone Marsan and Ralston
(1957) cite evidence gathered by Beck which suggests that in
most cases "the maximum degree of pressure against the
infant's head is directed to the left side during the process
of delivery. This then might result in a greater degree of
hippocampal herniation on that side, and a more severe left-
sided epileptogenic lesion" (Ajmone Marsan and Ralston, 1957,
p. 229). Although these authors were concerned with the
greater incidence of left-sided activation of seizures in
cases of bilateral temporal lobe epilepsy, the same considerations might apply to the higher incidence of left-sided
involvement of the temporal lobe in general.

[4] It is not entirely clear what contribution is made by subject-
ing animals with cerebral lesions to the enormous stress of the
free-ranging environment. The most that can be said is that
it demonstrates very dramatically the disability of an animal
prepared surgically in a particular way; at the least, it might
be viewed as an example of the complete triumph of the experimenter over the animal. I am indebted to Professor Joseph E.
Barmack for the latter phrase.

[5] Figure 1 is reprinted by permission of the American Psychological Association.

[6] Figure 4 is reprinted by permission of the American Psychological Association.

[7] Figure 5 is reprinted by permission of the N.Y. Academy of
Sciences.

References

Ajmone Marsan, C. and Ralston, B. L. The Epileptic Seizure.
    Illinois: Chas. C. Thomas, 1957.

Balasubramaniam, V. and Ramamurthi, B. Stereotaxic amygdal-
    otomy in behavior disorders. Confin. Neurol., 1970, 32,
    367-373.

Blumer, D. The temporal lobes and paroxysmal behavior dis-
    orders. Szondiana VII, 1967, 51, 273-285.

Chapman, W. P. Studies of the periamygdaloid area in relation
    to human behavior. In, H. C. Solomon, S. Cobb and W.
    Penfield (Eds.), The Brain and Human Behavior. Res. Pub.
    Assoc. Nerv. Ment. Dis., 36. Baltimore: Williams and
    Wilkins, 1958, 258-270.

Chitanondh, H. Stereotaxic amygdalotomy in the treatment of
    olfactory seizures and psychiatric disorders with olfac-
    tory hallucination. Confin. Neurol., 1966, 27, 181-196.

Crichton, M. The Terminal Man. New York: Alfred Knopf, 1972.

Delgado, Jose M. R. Aggression and defense under cerebral
    radio control. In, C. D. Clemente and D. B. Lindsley (Eds.),
    Aggression and Defense. Los Angeles: University of
    California Press, 1967, 171-193.

Falconer, M. A., Hill, D., Meyer, A. and Wilson, J. L. Clinical,
    radiological and EEG correlations with pathological changes
    in temporal lobe epilepsy and their significance in surgical
    treatment. In, M. Baldwin and P. Bailey, Temporal Lobe
    Epilepsy. Illinois: Chas. C. Thomas, 1958, 369-410.

Flynn, J. The neural basis of aggression in cats. In, D. C.
    Glass (Ed.), Neurophysiology and Emotion. New York:
    Rockefeller University Press, 1967, 40-60.

Franzen, E. A. and Myers, R. E. Neural control of social
    behavior: Prefrontal and anterior temporal cortex.
    Neuropsychologia, 1973, II, 141-157.

Gibbs, F. A. Ictal and non-ictal psychiatric disorders in
     temporal lobe epilepsy. J. Nerv. Ment. Dis., 1951, 113,
     522-528.

Gibbs, F. and Gibbs, E. Atlas of Electroencephalography.
     Boston: Addison Wesley, 1972.

Gloor, P. Discussion. In, C. D. Clemente and D. B. Lindsley
     (Eds.), Aggression and Defense. Los Angeles: University
     of California Press, 1967, 116-124.

Goldstein, Kurt. Human Nature in the Light of Psychopathology.
     Cambridge: Harvard University Press, 1940.

Goldstein, M. Brain research and violent behavior. Arch.
     Neurol., 1974, 30, 1-35.

Grunberg, F. and Pond, D. A. Conduct disorders in epileptic
     children. J. Neurol. Neurosurg. Psychiat., 1957, 20,
     65-68.

Gunn, J. and Bonn, J. Criminality and violence in epileptic
     prisoners. Brit. J. Psychiat., 1971, 118, 337-343.

Gunn, J. and Fenton, G. Epilepsy, automatism and crime. Lancet,
     1972, 1, 1173-1176.

Hill, D. Psychiatric disorders of epilepsy. Medical Press,
     1953, 229, 473-475.

Klüver, H. and Bucy, C. P. Preliminary analysis of functions
     of the temporal lobe. Arch. Neurol. and Psychiat., 1939,
     42, 979-1000.

Kling, A. Effects of amygdalectomy on social-affective behav-
     ior in non-human primates. In, B. E. Eleftheriou (Ed.),
     The Neurobiology of the Amygdala. New York: Plenum Press,
     1972, 511-536.

Kling, A., Lancaster, J., and Benitone, J. Amygdalectomy in
     the free ranging vervet (Cerocopithecus althiops). J.
     Psychiat. Res., 1970, 7, 191-199.

Kolb, L. C. Modern Clinical Psychiatry. Philadelphia: Saunders, 1973.

Mark, V. H. and Ervin, E. P. Violence and the Brain. New York: Harper and Row, 1970.

Milner, B. Laterality effects in audition. In, V. P. Mountcastle (Ed.), Interhemispheric Relations and Cerebral Dominance. Baltimore: The Johns Hopkins Press, 1962, 177-195.

Mirsky, A. F. Studies of the effects of brain lesions on social behavior in Macaca mulatta; methodological and theoretical considerations. Ann. N.Y. Acad. Sci., 1960, 85, 785-794.

Mirsky, A. F., Primac, D. W., Ajmone Marsan, C., Rosvold, H. E. and Stevens, J. A comparison of the psychological test performance of patients with focal and nonfocal epilepsy. Exp. Neurol., 1960, 2, 75-89.

Mirsky, A. F., Rosvold, H. E. and Pribram, K. H. Effects of cingulectomy on social behavior in monkeys. J. Neurophysiol., 1957, 20, 588-601.

Narabayashi, H., Nagao, T., Saito, Y., Yoshida, M. and Nagahata, M. Stereotaxic amygdalotomy for behavior disorders. Arch. Neurol., 1963, 9, 1-16.

Ounsted, C. Aggression and epilepsy rage in children with temporal lobe epilepsy. J. Psychosomatic Research, 1969, 13, 237-242.

Plotnik, R. Changes in social behavior of squirrel monkeys after anterior temporal lobectomy. J. Comp. and Physiol. Psychol., 1968, 66 (2), 369-377.

Redlich, F. C. and Freedman, D. X. The Theory and Practice of Psychiatry. New York: Basic Books, 1966.

Rey, J. H., Pond, D. A. and Evans, C. C. Clinical and electroencephalographic studies of temporal lobe function. Proceedings of the Royal Society of Medicine, 1949, XLII, 891-904.

Rodin, Ernst A. Psychomotor epilepsy and aggressive behavior.
    Arch. Gen. Psychiatry, 1972, 28, 210-213.

Rosvold, H. E., Mirsky, A. F. and Pribram, K. H. Influence of
    amygdalectomy on social behavior in monkeys. J. Comp.
    Physiol. Psychol., 1954, 47, 173-178.

Scoville, W. B. and Milner, B. Loss of recent memory after
    bilateral hippocampal lesions, J. Neurol. Neurosurg.
    Psychiat., 1957, 20, 11-21.

Serafetinides, E. A. Aggressiveness in temporal lobe epilep-
    tics and its relation to cerebral dysfunction and
    environmental factors. Epilepsia, 1965, 6, 33-42.

Small, J. G., Small, I. F. and Hayden, N, P. Further
    psychiatric investigations of patients with temporal and
    non-temporal lobe epilepsy, Amer. J. Psychiat., 1966, 123,
    3.

Stevens, J. R. Psychiatric Implications of psychomotor
    epilepsy. Arch. Gen. Psychiatry, 1966, 14, 461-471.

Sweet, W. H., Ervin, F. and Mark, V, H. The relationship of
    violent behavior to focal cerebral disease. In, S.
    Garattini and E. Siggs (Eds.), Aggressive Behavior. New
    York: John Wiley and Sons, 1969, 336-352.

Taylor, D. C. Aggression and Epilepsy. J. Psychosomatic
    Research, 1969, 13, 229-236.

Valenstein, E. S. Brain Control. New York: John Wiley and
    Sons, 1973.

Walker, E. A. and Blumer, D. Long term effects of temporal
    lobe lesions on sexual behavior and aggressivity. In,
    W. Fields and W. Sweet (Eds.), The Neurobiology of Violence.
    St. Louis: Warren Green (In press).

PARTICIPANTS

Speakers

Dr. Gray Eaton
Oregon Regional Primate Research Center
Beaverton, Oregon

Dr. John Flynn
Department of Psychiatry
Yale University
New Haven, Connecticut

Dr. John Harvey
Department of Psychology
University of Iowa
Iowa City, Iowa

Dr. Gary Lynch
Department of Psychobiology
University of California
Irvine, California

Dr. Gerald McClearn
Institute of Behavioral Genetics
University of Colorado
Boulder, Colorado

Dr. Allan Mirsky
Department of Psychiatry
Boston University
Boston, Massachusetts

Dr. Ashley Montagu
Princeton, New Jersey

Dr. Manuol Penna
Department of Psychiatry
University of Maryland
Baltimore, Maryland

Dr. Adrian Perachio
Yerkes Regional Primate Research Center
Atlanta, Georgia

Dr. Richard E. Whalen
Department of Psychobiology
University of California
Irvine, California

Visiting Scholars:

Dr. David Adams	Wesleyan University
Dr. Marylynn Barkley	University of Connecticut
Dr. Annette Erlich	California State University, Los Angeles
Dr. Rod Gorney	University of California, Los Angeles
Dr. Seymour Kessler	Stanford University
Dr. Melvin King	State University of New York, Cortland
Dr. Alan Leshner	Bucknell University
Dr. Sandra Molenauer	California State University, San Diego
Dr. Klaus Miczek	Carnegie-Mellon University
Dr. Rod Plotnick	California State University, San Diego
Dr. Michael Potegal	New York State Psychiatric Institution
Dr. Donald Powell	University of South Carolina
Dr. Frank Rowe	Illinois Institute of Technology
Dr. Douglas Smith	University of Connecticut

Department of Psychobiology
University of California, Irvine

Faculty

Cotman, Carl W.
Giolli, Roland A.
Globus, Albert
Josephson, Robert K.
Killackey, Herbert P.
Lynch, Gary S.
McGaugh, James L.

Noble, Ernest P.
Starr, Arnold
Verzeano, Marcel
Waymire, Jack C.
Weinberger, Norman M.
Whalen, Richard E.
Yahr, Pauline I.

Representing NIMH:

Dr. Lyle Bivens
Dr. Leonard Lash
Dr. George Renaud

INDEX

Aborigines, Australian, 17
Acetylcholine, 127
Acetylcholinesterase, 107,117
Aggression
  Birds, 55
  Cat, 54,75
  Human, 1, 165, 185
  Inhibition of, 24, 76, 175
  Isolation induced, 56
  Pain induced, 56
  Primate, 6, 33, 54, 69, 194
  Rodent, 55, 89, 150
  Territorial, 56
Alcohol, 173

Brain
  Chemical stimulation, 138
  Electrical activity, 79, 185
  Electrical stimulation, 66, 126, 178
  Enzymes, 133
  Hormonal stimulation, 154, 177
  Lesions, 54, 100, 125, 178, 195
  Transmitters, 95, 126
Bushmen, 10, 31

Defense, 53
Dopamine, 132
Drugs, 142
  Alcohol, 173
  Lithium, 177
  Stimulants, 177, 183
  Tranquilizers, 176

Electroconvulsive therapy, 178
Eskimos, 14

Fink-Heimer technique, 100, 114

Gatherer-hunters, 2, 4
Genes, 87

Histochemistry
  Acetylcholinesterase, 105
  Fluorescence, 132
  Horseradish peroxidase, 111
  Iodonitrotetrazolium, 105
Hormones, 79, 149
Horseradish peroxidase, 111, 118

Hunting, 6
Hyperkinesis,   169, 183

Inbred strains, 88
Indians, 22
Iodonitrotetrazolium,   105, 116
Islanders,
  Andaman, 19
  Pitcairn, 23

Lithium, 177

Methodology
  Animal behavior, 34, 71
  Autoradiography, 110
  Brain lesions, 54, 100, 125,
   178, 195
  Brain stimulation
   chemical, 138
   electrical, 66, 126, 178
   hormonal, 154
  Electrical recording, 79, 185
  Endocrine, 149
  Neuroanatomy, 99
  Stereotaxic, 67
Motivation, 63

Norepinephrine,   132

Predation,   58, 62
Pygmies, 16

Serotonin, 132
Sex differences, 50
Stimulants,   177, 183

Tasaday, 3, 20
Tasmanians, 9
Testosterone, 150
Threat, 38
Tranquilizers, 176
Transmitters, 95, 127

Violence
  and alcohol, 172

Weapons, 1, 172

XYY snydrome, 98